KEEN ON RETIREMENT

KEEN

on

RETIREMENT

Engineering the Second Half of Your Life

BILL KEEN

KEEN ON RETIREMENT

Engineering the Second Half of Your Life

ISBN 978-1-5445-0183-3 *Hardcover*

978-1-5445-0181-9 *Paperback*

978-1-5445-0182-6 *Ebook*

978-1-5445-0184-0 *Audiobook*

To all of the clients I've had the privilege of serving over the years. Thank you for demonstrating that through hard work, character, and responsibility, it is possible to start from nothing and build a fulfilling retirement for you and your families.

CONTENTS

INTRODUCTION

You've worked a full-time job for thirty to forty years, and you're used to getting a regular paycheck. At this point, you probably operate on professional autopilot. Much of your time is accounted for. You work *at least* forty hours a week—it's your routine. You've grown used to it.

All of that is about to change. Retirement is approaching, and soon those regular paychecks will stop showing up in your mailbox or bank account. Your sense of financial security may well be challenged. The transition can be dramatic and, if you're unprepared, extremely difficult.

Or maybe you've already retired, and you're in the midst of making the adjustment to this new phase of your life. You're looking for someone to help you on the journey.

The truth is most people start their retirement planning

with little to no assets or investments. Throughout their careers, hopefully they've lived within their means, made prudent financial decisions, and tried to save. Now the reality is hitting them that they need to create a new source of income for their retirement years. It's not enough to merely save and accumulate money; they have to become more thoughtful investors as they will soon be in the distribution phase of their investing lifetimes. They're going to live off that money for the rest of their lives.

It can be difficult for people to wrap their minds around this change. This is why it's so important to put a solid plan in place to successfully navigate the transition. There may be many ways to be successful, and you might be able to achieve it in some other way. The plan I share with you in this book has worked for my clients over the years.

TIME IS RUNNING OUT

A good portion of the clients I've worked with have been career engineers. In fact, engineers or employees of engineering firms make up approximately 60 percent of all the clients at my firm Keen Wealth Advisors. They come to us for advice because they are planners by nature. They understand that it takes years of thinking, planning, and preparing to even begin to get a big project off the ground.

They also have vast expertise in their fields, so they understand what it means to be specialists. They are fully aware that when it comes to retirement planning, they *know* what they *don't know*, and they're willing to seek advice.

As retirement approaches, they've begun to realize just how different life is going to be, and they have a limited amount of time to ensure that everything is lined up correctly to prepare for it. In fact, they only have one chance with the resources they have accumulated, so they can't afford to make any major mistakes. Realizing this, they look for specialized help, so they can get it right.

Time is a priceless commodity, and, not to be morbid, there's an end date for each of us. The years go by increasingly fast, so we shouldn't wait to get our affairs in order. Beyond retirement, you want to ensure that your spouse or children are taken care of, that they won't be taken advantage of by an unscrupulous advisor, broker, or salesperson—or even a scam artist or disingenuous future spouse—when you're gone.

Trying to navigate all the complexities of tax law, estate planning, investment rules, and finances on your own, along with all the emotions involved, can become a full-time job, yet the whole point of retirement is to not have to work so hard anymore. You need to put a plan in place that allows you to delegate this work.

AVOIDING EMOTIONAL MISTAKES

When you're first starting out in your career and trying to build wealth, it's easy to make bad investment decisions, especially when you have a limited perspective on the markets and economy. Maybe you've learned some hard lessons along the way, but with retirement drawing near, you can no longer afford to make major mistakes.

The news media loves to announce that the world's coming to an end anytime the market is off by a few points in a day. Investors who lack the training or coaching to put this volatility into perspective are prone to make emotional decisions about their investments that can prove to be catastrophic. The most common emotional mistake people make is to sell their investments at a bottom in the market. Another mistake is to over-invest in the latest fad.

Often, when the market goes through a correction and experiences a downturn, people feel scared and get out of the market entirely. Then they find themselves sitting out while the market rebounds by 30, 50, 100, 200 percent or much more. I've spoken to individuals who got out of the market in 2009 and never got back in. Meanwhile, the market has rebounded by over 380 percent from March 2009 through March 2019 with dividends reinvested since the recession, and in these cases, they have cost themselves seven figures.[1] That's the damage an emotional decision can make to your long-term financial well-being.

Other times, people see a news story promoting some stock or industry, and they believe the hype. They buy in heavily without understanding how the specific investment fits into their financial plan. It's a spur-of-the-moment decision, and it can cost them a lot.

You can't afford to make these kinds of mistakes at this stage in your life. You need someone who can see around the corners, helping you develop a disciplined process that will ideally help you take advantage of market volatility while keeping you smartly allocated.

You're going to be *somewhere* financially during your journey in retirement. The question is, will your journey be with discernment and intentionality, or will it be random?

PUTTING A PLAN IN PLACE

When we talk about making a financial plan, we're talking about creating a living, breathing roadmap that deals with

1 "March 4, 2009-March 4, 2019," *StockCharts*, https://stockcharts.com/freecharts/perf.php?$SPXTR.

every component of your retirement, taking into account all spending needs, rules and regulations, Social Security, wills and trusts, healthcare, and taxes.

The engine to that plan is the investments you make in accordance with your individual considerations, bearing in mind what those investments need to produce for you and your family in the form of income and growth over time—coupled with your tolerance for risk and volatility.

Rough times are inevitable, and there will be turbulence along the way. You will deal with illness, market corrections and disturbances, possibly job loss or other unfortunate events. As they say, when it rains, it pours, so you need a plan that will help you weather these challenges. You don't want to find yourself scrambling or responding emotionally. With a plan in place, you can sit back calmly and say, "Here are the things I've already committed myself to, and here are the goals I know I want to achieve. I don't have to let this current problem derail my thinking. My advisory team has my plan and is looking out for me."

We see so much anxiety in people as retirement approaches—a fear of uncertainty, a concern about the unknown—but once clients have a plan in place, it's amazing the difference it makes. Six months to a year after retirement, when they've successfully navigated the transition and realize the plan is working, they seem ten years younger.

They find themselves sleeping better at night, feeling healthier and happier than they have in a while. Often, they describe the retirement years as the best part of life. They have wisdom and experience from their decades in a successful career. Not only can they appreciate everything they've been through, but they can relax and look ahead to rewarding years made possible by a life of discipline and persistence. They have the capital, resources, and financial security to pursue the passions, health, hobbies, and family time they've always dreamed of.

As their financial advisor, seeing clients enjoy a successful retirement is one of the most rewarding parts of my professional life.

COMMON DANGERS AND OPPORTUNITIES

In twenty-seven years of professional experience, I've conducted over fifteen thousand private meetings with clients. I've seen the planning and investment strategies that work, the most common dangers people face, and the opportunities that exist in their lives and in the markets. I've observed the recurring themes and the mistakes people make.

In this book, I want to clearly and succinctly describe the

things I've seen working for people over the years, as well as the dangers that can derail your retirement plans.

When I first started in this industry, many people still depended on their pensions to see them through retirement, but even then, the paradigm had begun to change. Today, very few people have pensions or any other monthly income stream they can depend on. Though most people will receive Social Security, rarely is it enough to cover everything they need. Retirement planning and long-term security can simply no longer be entrusted to the government or corporate employers. More than ever, the responsibility lies with the individual to plan and prepare.

I believe it's a good idea to have a financial advisor you trust and respect who can hold you accountable. A good advisor will help you clarify what you want your retirement life to look like in all aspects, and they will help you get there. They will guide you in developing your budget, show you how to pay the least amount of legally required taxes, and provide accountability to keep you on track.

Unfortunately, all advisors are not equal, and some simply don't have the experience to deal with every individual situation. Others lack introspection or might have ulterior motives. That's why it's so important to find a team with experience, depth, and the credentials that you can trust.

MAKE THE MOST OF YOUR RETIREMENT

Individuals tend to fall into one of two categories. First, there are those who take responsibility for their future. Then, there are those who, either consciously or unconsciously, believe that someone else will take care of them, but we've found that, in this day and age, that mentality doesn't produce fruit for the future.

My goal is to help you take responsibility for your long-term success. You don't need to be a CFP®, CPA, or estate planning attorney, but it's helpful to gain financial literacy. I believe everyone deserves to be financially secure, and, more importantly, I believe everyone *can* be financially secure. I want you to gain a sense of confidence in your future, so you can live with peace of mind about your retirement.

Life isn't going to be bliss all the time, but if you plan well and live within that plan, you may find yourself experiencing a sense of freedom. Happiness in retirement doesn't require having millions of dollars, though it can certainly help. I've met people who live on nothing but their social security who are perfectly happy. They are enjoying hobbies like gardening or social activities and going to church, and they have confidence because they live smartly within their means.

The key is to plan well and stick to your plan. Unfortunately, many people are mired in debt, and without putting a spending plan in place, they will enter retirement in a dangerous state.

Others have built wealth over a lifetime, saving and investing, diversifying, navigating market cycles, and staying the course. As a result, they are poised for many years of peace and happiness, provided they back it up with a secure retirement plan.

Whatever your present financial condition, this book will help you design a plan to meet your retirement goals. It will show you how to create a financial engine to support the lifestyle you desire. On these pages you'll find the information you need to make the most of your retirement.

PART ONE

DRAW THE PLAN

Chapter One

ASSESS YOUR ASSETS

When I was ten years old, I lived with my father in a tiny apartment in Kansas City. He had worked nights for years, but it was a rough job market at the time, and he soon found himself unemployed due to company downsizing. Every day he was filled with anxiety over finances, and I was very aware of that anxiety. I experienced his fear as well as we waited for his unemployment check to arrive. In those days, checks weren't direct deposited. You had to cross your fingers and hope that it showed up in the mailbox on time.

I remember very well how he struggled to make ends meet. He was a loving father who would have done anything for me. I was the center of his world, but the stress and strain over finances consumed our lives. I become a pro at preparing Kraft Macaroni and Cheese that year. We could only afford to use the laundromat every other week, so we often washed our clothes in the sink or bathtub. One of my fondest memories was being able to buy our lunch at a local hamburger place called Andy's Malt Shop with a few dollars I had saved.

This experience gave me the determination to understand finances, so by the time I was fourteen, I'd made up my mind to earn a finance degree in college. I was determined that I would be able to provide for my father so that one day he could be at rest from financial fear and anxiety. I would never again struggle as my father had struggled.

Despite the hardships, my childhood wasn't unhappy. I had a great-aunt, Nina, born in 1901, who was a source of constant comfort and counsel. She was the personnel director—a rare position for a woman in those days—for a well-known department store in Kansas City called Emery, Bird, Thayer from the 1930s until it closed in 1968. She introduced me to the markets when I was a child. She owned shares of stock in the Russell Stover candy company, because she actually knew Russell Stover himself.

Great-Aunt Nina meets with executives from Emily, Bird, Thayer

NINA K. SCHANTZ

PERSONNEL DIRECTOR
EMERY, BIRD, THAYER
KANSAS CITY, MO.

I remember she would buy the *Wall Street Journal* every day so she could track the markets, and she would often tell me what was going on. I would visit her regularly at her apartment on the Country Club Plaza here in Kansas City, and she would take me shopping for school clothes and even suits as I got older. She gave me etiquette training and provided me unconditional love and confidence in my future. She also proved to be a valuable resource for me on many fronts, and I was able to repay her as I handled her finances and helped her get the care she needed during her later years. Great-aunt Nina passed away in 2001 at the age of 100, but I still think of her often.

Ultimately, my childhood ambition wasn't materialistic. Despite the financial hardships, I didn't dream about being wealthy. My parents were divorced, and I spent time with both of them. I watched them struggle with finances, and I just wanted them to be happy. I'd absorbed much of their stress, developed insecurity about money, and had lingering fear about losing everything. I didn't want to suffer as my parents had suffered, and I wanted to take care of them as well.

When I finally achieved success, I supported both of them. My father passed away in 2001 at the age of sixty from lung cancer. Prior to that, however, from 1999 to 2000, he worked for me when I was running Keen Wealth as a group within a larger brokerage firm. When I would introduce him to clients, I would say, "This is Mr. Keen of Keen Wealth." I think many people assumed he had founded the firm, and I worked for him. I didn't correct them. After all of the financial struggles he'd experienced,

I relished the opportunity to provide my father with some dignity in the latter years of his life.

My father loved me dearly and taught me many life skills that I use to this day. He was the most fun and sincere guy that anyone could know. Yes, there was financial stress and strain, but I regret none of my childhood hardships. I wouldn't trade them for anything because they gave me a clear purpose in life. Here I am many years later helping others to achieve their own financial security.

My mother is still alive, and we have a great relationship. I also have a stepmother who provided me much support, love, and guidance who is also living today. We, too, have a special bond for which I am grateful. In a way, my childhood anxieties gave me the drive I needed to succeed. I decided that failure simply wasn't an option. No matter what, I was going to figure out how to be financially secure so I could provide for my family.

INSPIRED TO HELP OTHERS

Those early experiences inspired me to help other people get their finances in order. I love empowering people to take responsibility for their finances and, ultimately, their retirement. The desire to do so myself is what led me to pursue a finance degree in college.

After college, I worked at a prominent mutual fund company in Kansas City, Twentieth Century Investors (later called American Century Investment Management), founded by James E. Stowers Jr. in 1958. Mr. Stowers founded the firm with an objective to help investors achieve financial independence, including those who were just starting out.

For me, it was a dream to work in Mr. Stowers' organization as I had tremendous respect for him. After all, he had created one of the most respected and successful financial institutions in the country. In addition, he and his wife, Virginia, endowed the Stowers Institute for Medical Research, setting the ultimate example of how financial success can be a force for good, giving "Hope for Life." They have since donated *billions* of dollars to the Institute, and it is considered one of the best biological research institutions in the world.

In my role at the company, I primarily entered data on new account forms and processed client requests. I interacted with clients but only to ensure that specific data on the forms was correct. I took orders but was not authorized to give specific investment advice or guidance. Although I was very early in my career, I was licensed, and I was able to see that in many cases clients were making emotional or uninformed investment decisions. However, we were an investment manager, not an advisor. The clients needed to retain an advisor elsewhere. Today, American Century offers advisory services.

As an employee, I was graded on how quickly and accurately I could enter data, and while I was grateful for the experience and the values the firm instilled in me, it didn't take long to realize I needed to pursue my passion of advising clients directly on their planning and investing. About a year after starting my job at Twentieth Century, I cold-walked into every brokerage firm in town, eventually leading to a local Dean Witter office. With no prior contact, I asked for a job and was hired on the spot.

Standing in the lobby of World Trade Center South Tower in 1993.

At the time, I had no assets, no family money, no connections, no influence, and I didn't know anyone else who had those things either. I was handed a phone book and given an inspirational speech: "Kid, you're probably not going to make it. One in fifty survive here, but we have to hire a certain number of people, so we're giving you a shot. Good luck."

The next few years were like a cross between the first half of the movie *Wall Street* (before Bud Fox goes bad) and the movie *The Pursuit of Happyness*. In fact, I have posters of those movies on the wall in my family room to this day—they hit very close to home.

I wound up training in the Dean Witter office on the 83rd floor of the South Tower of the World Trade Center in New York. In fact, I was working there just a month after the towers were attacked for the first time in 1993. You might remember that incident. A terrorist drove a Ryder truck into the parking garage beneath the World Trade

Center and detonated a bomb. As you can imagine, those were hectic days.

For the next twenty years, I worked in several Wall Street firms, and it gradually became clear to me that there were inherent conflicts of interest, especially in bank-owned brokerage firms. Many of those conflicts of interest came to light during the financial collapse of 2008, when the public first learned about all of the low-quality mortgage products that had been aggressively pushed to retail clients. This kind of thing had been going on for years, brokerage firms pushing products in order to make fast profits.

I spent many years building my financial planning practice inside of the bank brokerage world, but I knew that remaining in that culture wasn't my long-term goal. On the contrary, I had dreamed of being in a firm that was focused on long-term financial planning rather than a firm that constantly cross-sold products like mortgages and credit cards. Although I didn't participate in the cross-selling, it was still uncomfortable.

In 2008 and 2009, the parent company of the firm I worked for went through tremendous difficulty, and suddenly we found ourselves answering for the highly questionable moves the parent company had been making. Every day, those decisions made the headlines, and the environment became insufferable.

Finally, I decided that it was time to realize my dream of operating my own independent, registered investment advisory firm, acting as a fiduciary. It took almost six years to make it happen, but I finally founded Keen Wealth Advisors in 2014.

THE BEST HALF OF YOUR LIFE

My parents were ill-prepared for what should have been the best half of their lives, because they were unable to provide for their own retirement. I see this same problem in the lives of many people. This is why I do what I do. I want to help people become financially literate, so they can live without anxiety and prepare for a comfortable retirement—even if they are starting with nothing.

Achieving a comfortable retirement isn't only possible for movie stars, lottery winners, successful professional athletes, or the wealthy few. So-called "normal" people have a hard time believing they can reach a point in their lives where they no longer have to work, but I've dedicated my life to making it a reality. It's why I get up in the morning, why I look forward to every day, and why I created my firm.

I always root for the underdog. When you start with nothing, you really have to fight against the culture of consumerism and instant gratification in order to save and invest for long-term comfort. You have to learn discipline and patience, which can be difficult, but it's possible. It's possible for just about anyone.

I believe everyone deserves to retire with peace of mind about their finances, to live out the second half of their lives without anxiety and strife. Money is a contributing factor to fear, anxiety, and stress. It breaks up marriages and causes all kinds of health problems. Maybe you've already seen the detrimental effects of money problems in your own life. The good news is, by using a few basic tools, you can build the life you deserve, no matter where you're starting from.

I'm a professional financial advisor, but I'm also a pilot. Though they might not seem at first glance to have much in common, both pilots and financial advisors make life-or-death decisions every day. One bad decision while you're up in the air can lead to catastrophe. In a similar way, if you make a bad decision at retirement age, you don't have forty more years to make up for it.

The problem is, no matter your career, you're going to deal with retirement in some respect, so you have to become as knowledgeable about retirement as you can. Even if you plan to never retire because you love what you do, you still need to prepare for the possibility of illness forcing a retirement. In a sense, retirement planning becomes your new career, and you're going to have to deal with the investing, taxes, Social Security, Medicare, estate planning, changing family dynamics, and so much more. One bad decision can create a domino effect.

Though everyone has to deal with retirement, there's very little training out there for non-financial professionals. Most people turn to the headlines. They get baited into seminars offering free steak dinners that are intended to hard-sell them on some equity index annuity. This isn't a real financial education.

Most people simply don't know where to turn for independent, objective financial information, and they don't have the time to go back to college and earn a finance degree. Even if they go back to college, degree programs often fail to teach practical advice for retirement planning. Employers typically don't train their people to prepare for retirement either. They might provide a few options, but they don't give advice about which ones to choose, because they don't want the liability, and, frankly, don't have the expertise.

The Social Security Administration will also tell you about various retirement options, but they're not going to tell you which one is the best fit for you and your lifestyle. Where else can you turn? Either you have to make retirement planning your new full-time job, or you have to find an advisor who is committed to providing you with the information you need to make educated financial decisions. They will help bring all of the relevant pieces together to create a plan that fits your needs, preferences, and retirement goals, so you can enjoy your retirement.

YOUR HISTORY WITH MONEY

Whenever I speak to someone about making a plan for the next phase of their life, the first step I ask them to take is to gain clarity about where they currently stand. You can't begin the journey until you know where you are, and you need to understand how you got there. That means revisiting how you grew up, particularly the financial circumstances of your upbringing and your resulting relationship with money. What was the family dynamic? What part of the country did you grow up in? Where did you go to school? Were you an only child, first child, middle child, or last child? Did your family have money, or did they struggle?

The circumstances of your upbringing have shaped your relationship with money, and by examining it in depth, you can gain a better sense of what you're dealing with and some of the challenges you will face. If you're married, you will want to reach this same level of understanding about your spouse. Once you've done that, you can begin to explore your options.

INVENTORY OF ASSETS

At this point, you want to create an inventory of assets, so you know exactly what you have to work with. Do you have an estate plan in place? Is there a will or trust? Even if you don't have the documents yet, have you at least thought through these things? If something were to happen to you, what would become of your spouse or children?

If you use a tax professional to prepare your taxes every year, you want to take a look at how your taxes come together. In particular, look for anything unusual. Do you have any assets like a farm or outside business? Have you sponsored or provided a personal guarantee for an outside business of one of your children? That could be either an asset or a liability, but it will be a factor either way.

Next, you want to take into account the Social Security you have earned for yourself, your spouse, and your family. We will dig into the importance of Social Security in a later chapter, so you can learn how to maximize your benefits. You will also want to take into account a qualified retirement plan, if you have one, as well as any IRAs, brokerage accounts, CDs, or money market accounts. What has your thinking and planning been about emergency funds?

You also want to look at non-monetary assets, such as your reputation and network of friends or colleagues. These are assets during your career, and they should continue to be assets into your retirement, as your network provides a place to plug in socially in order to maintain an active and engaging lifestyle. Your health can be either an asset or a liability, depending on how well you've taken care of yourself.

INVENTORY OF LIABILITIES

In this day and age, there are more young people in their

twenties living at home than ever before. Often, it's simply a "failure to launch." However, when a parent is trying to support an adult child while also preparing for their own retirement, they often compromise their own retirement plan. If that's your situation, then you will have to consider implementing healthy boundaries. Of course, as parents, we will do just about anything for our children, but there comes a point where helping your kids can actually end up hurting your kids.

This is a kind of liability that people don't always think about. Other kinds of liabilities are obvious. How much debt have you accrued? For example, how much do you owe on your house? Do you have any credit card debt or consumer debt? If there's consumer debt, you will want to get a handle on it quickly because when you retire, you will be living on a fixed income.

In our culture, people have gotten used to living with credit card debt, but it's likely to be in your best interest to pay it off well before retirement. I often work with clients to create a plan for eliminating debt by making a tax-smart withdrawal from their retirement account or after-tax account. It's worth it to stop the high interest rate on credit card debt.

Loans are also a very common liability. You might have a car loan. Maybe you cosigned for student loans for your children or grandchildren. As I mentioned, we've found that many people sign for business loans for their children. If that's your situation, you need to consider the depths of your liability. If you're a personal guarantor on a business loan, you can lose a lot more than you may be aware of, so you will want to get a handle on the risk.

YOUR RETIREMENT BLUEPRINT

Once you've gathered the facts about your assets and liabilities, it's time to figure out what your specific retirement objectives are. You would never build a building without a blueprint, and you would never fly in a commercial airliner without a flight plan filed. It is absolutely essential to get this right because one mistake in that blueprint or flight plan can produce a cascade of problems that can be devastating. In the same way, you can't prepare for your retirement without a retirement blueprint.

As I like to say, what gets measured gets done. Creating a blueprint gives you a basis for measuring how you're doing in preparing for retirement and beyond. By establishing objectives, setting goals, and creating a timeline, you can gauge how you're doing. As part of that blueprint, you also want to make room for the unexpected. You can't control everything, after all, and when problems arise in life that are outside of your control, you want to avoid having to rethink your entire blueprint. However, it is on you to, at a minimum, "control the controllable."

Of course, a retirement blueprint can still become outdated fairly quickly because life continues to change along the way. For that reason, we encourage people to update their blueprint at least once a year or anytime a major event happens in your life.

A MINDSET FOR YOUR BLUEPRINT

I've helped thousands of people make the transition from working to retirement with the freedom, flexibility, and resources to realize their vision for the retirement life they've always wanted. Many of them grew up with very little, but they worked long and hard in their careers, saved, and made prudent decisions. Once they are able to retire and live independently wealthy, it almost seems like a dream.

Most people become conscious of their retirement needs in their mid-fifties. Suddenly, it hits them that there is coming a point where they won't have to get up and go to work anymore. Even if they enjoy their jobs, they begin to visualize what this post-retirement life might look like.

I like to encourage people to think positively by telling them, "The best is yet to come." Admittedly, some find this hard to believe. "That sounds great," they reply, "but I'm fifty-five, and I already have aches and pains. How can you tell me the best is yet to come?"

"You have acquired wisdom from the journey," I reply. "You have resources, and hopefully you've made a lot of mistakes—because we learn from mistakes, whether they are about relationships, time, health, or finances. You can now approach the next phase of your life with all of this wisdom and all of these resources."

I always encourage people to spend deliberate time thinking about what they want their retirement to look like. If you're married, this should be a conversation you also have with your spouse. Get intentional about where you want to be three years, five years, ten years, and twenty years from now. Just start thinking about it and discussing it.

To create your blueprint, take a piece of paper or a whiteboard and write down how old you will be at each of those intervals—three, five, ten, and twenty years. Also write down how old your spouse and children will be. This can help take your mind away from the minutiae of the day and put it into the future. What do you want your life to look like at each interval? Ideally, where will you be physically, financially, mentally, spiritually? What is your ideal future? Don't leave any of your hopes and dreams out of this discussion. Include it all in your blueprint.

Life can—and will—throw you curveballs, but when you visualize where you want to be and write it down, you'll be ready with a design of your ideal life. Some people feel guilty about doing this, and others think it's a bit corny, but in my experience it works.

We had a client who retired from a major engineering firm that we spent seven years coaching and counseling about his upcoming retirement. He'd actually set a date for his retirement when he started his career in his twenties, laying out when he would retire, at what age, and what assets he would have. His vision for his future guided his decision-making throughout his career, and he ultimately retired according to plan, within six months of the retirement date he'd envisioned nearly forty years earlier.

Once you're conscious about what you want, you can begin to reverse engineer your life going forward. Remember, this isn't about what your kids want for you. This isn't about what your financial advisor thinks you should be doing, or what the culture says you should be doing. At this point, it's all about what *you* want. You get one shot at life, so what do you want?

YOUR BLUEPRINT IS ABOUT MORE THAN MONEY

Remember, your future isn't just about money. It's about

the social life you want to have in retirement. Many of our clients want to become engaged in their church or religious communities. They plan to go on mission trips or volunteer on charitable boards.

This is important because sometimes spouses get a little stir-crazy when they're suddenly around each other all the time. They said, "For better or for worse, 'til death do us part," but not for breakfast, lunch, *and* dinner—it's frequently too much. We'll talk about maintaining your marriage during retirement in depth in a later chapter, but for now, begin thinking about the social life you want to have. It's important to get out there and find meaningful activity to be a part of. This becomes a big part of your *why*.

I know of one gentleman who loves triathlons. He's now seventy-nine years old, and he regularly participates in races all over the Midwest. He also volunteers at the local museum as a docent and donates his time giving tours several times a week.

I know others who have traveled the world in their retirement. Some buy RVs, so they can tour the country. They relish the freedom of going where they want to go at any time. They relish no longer having to spend time with people they don't want to spend time with, such as coworkers or neighbors. This level of freedom can be empowering.

Ultimately, it's about creating a clear vision for the future that *you* want. This becomes a blueprint for your retirement, so you can begin to put a plan in place to make it happen. Next, you have to figure out how you're going to fund that vision.

Chapter Two

RETIREMENT ACCOUNTS

Most people who are planning for retirement put their wealth into "qualified plans," such as a 401k (for private sector employees), 403b (for nonprofit and public education employees), and 457 plans (for state and municipal employees). Federal employees also have something called the Thrift Savings Plan.

When someone approaches retirement, they have the option of moving their funds from a qualified plan into an IRA (Individual Retirement Account). This allows them to maintain tax deferral, withdrawing the money as needed. They only pay taxes on the money they pull out.

Since an IRA will probably play an important role in your retirement planning, I want to provide you with an overview of what they are, how they got started, and how they work. I also want to provide you with the information you need to use your IRA in the most tax-efficient way, both now and when you hit retirement. We'll start with a little background to lay the groundwork.

IT'S NOT YOUR PARENTS' RETIREMENT

The way people retire today is very different from the way people retired in previous generations. In your parents' generation, people would typically work for thirty-five to forty years, while their employer assumed the financial risk for funding their retirement. The employer put money away for each employee's pension plan, so that when people retired after a long career, they had a guaranteed lifelong income.

A pension plan is called a "defined benefit plan," meaning there is a formula for determining how much you receive for your monthly payments for life, typically based on your five highest years of salary, your age, and years of service. In some instances, employees can choose to take the money as a lump sum, but rules vary.

Today, defined benefit plans have largely been replaced by defined contribution plans, which means, in most cases, employers will match employee contributions to a qualified plan, such as a 401k. Some companies offer profit-sharing plans as well, where they put even more into employee contribution plans based on the profitability of the firm. Finally, some companies offer an Employee Stock Ownership Plan commonly referred to as an ESOP.

This is the reality of retirement today, and whichever plan your employer offers, you are going to have more responsibility for contributing to and managing your own retirement income than your parents' generation did.

LOOKING BACK ON MODERN RETIREMENT

In 1875, the American Express company created the first private pension plan in the US for elderly workers and workers with disabilities. By 1926, shortly before the onset of the Great Depression, there were approximately two hundred private pension plans that had been established by large employers across the country. Of course, life expectancy was much shorter then, so funding a person's retirement wasn't as onerous as it is today. An employee might retire at sixty-five and then live another five or ten years, but today, it's not unusual for retirees to live another twenty or thirty years.

IRAs, or Individual Retirement Accounts, were created in 1974 by the Employee Retirement Income Security Act. Initially, the government allowed people to put up to $1,500 a year into these accounts, though that amount has increased quite a bit since then. Money put into an

IRA was typically deductible from income taxes, and as the money grew, it was tax-deferred. Taxes were paid only when money was withdrawn from the account. Often, employers matched employee contributions, which also grew tax deferred.

In 1978, with the country reeling from staggering inflation and other economic woes, Congress passed the Revenue Act of 1978, which cleared the way for the establishment of many defined contribution plans, including the 401k. In 1997, the late Senator William Roth of Delaware created legislation to establish Roth IRAs. His idea was to create an IRA for after-tax money, so instead of receiving a tax deduction on money put into the account, the money is taxed initially but then allowed to grow tax-free forever, even when it is withdrawn.

There are actually two ways to put money into a Roth IRA. The first is to make ongoing annual contributions. The other way is to take an existing traditional IRA and convert it into a Roth IRA. You trigger the initial tax payment on any pretax dollars coming from the IRA, but then the money grows tax-free forever. That makes it very appealing to many people.

Because of this, brokerage firms in 1997 and 1998 were telling people to convert *all* of their IRAs into Roth IRAs. The government liked this because it meant they received a lot of tax revenue right away, instead of having to wait until people retired.

Of course, converting everything to a Roth IRA carries the risk of pushing you into a higher tax bracket. Furthermore, when the tech bubble burst between 2000 and 2002, the up-front tax cost of these conversions became a problem. If you'd converted $1 million into a Roth IRA at that time, you first paid taxes on it, and then you lost a lot of the money when the market tanked—a double hit that hurt many people who had listened to the advice of brokers. It was so bad that the government began allowing people to get their tax money back and reinvest it back into the IRA as if it had never been converted. In fact, this do-over lasted until 2017, when it was taken away.

NAVIGATING YOUR OPTIONS

That brings us to today. We now have numerous tools we can work with to prepare for retirement. It's important to understand exactly what your company offers, so you can maximize your retirement options. Make sure you understand the rules about putting money into and taking money out of these qualified retirement plans.

ROTH IRAS AND TRADITIONAL IRAS

Generally speaking, you need to wait until you are fifty-nine-and-a-half to take money out of an IRA, unless you meet certain criteria, or you will pay a 10 percent penalty on your withdrawal. Remember, anytime you take pre-tax money out of a qualified plan or traditional IRA, you're going to pay taxes in the year you take it out, which will impact your tax bracket. The exception is a Roth IRA, in which there are no taxes due after the initial payment. However, you still have to have had a Roth opened for at least five years and be at least fifty-nine-and-a-half, or else the growth will be taxed and potentially penalized. That's why we often tell parents to fund Roth IRAs for their children. They are a powerful retirement tool with a lot of built-in flexibility.

With a traditional IRA, when you reach seventy-and-a-half, you have to begin taking a required minimum distribution. This means you are required to take a specific dollar amount out of the account each year, which is calculated based on the value of the account at the end of the previous year, your age, and a life-expectancy table. The government has created this requirement because they don't want to wait forever for their taxes on the money. This also applies to balances in your employer's qualified plans, but not while you are still working.

If you're going to include a traditional IRA or qualified plan in your retirement plan, you have to take the required minimum distributions into account. In some cases, retirees are taking more than the minimum anyway, so they aren't affected by the rule, at least initially. However, failing to take out the minimum distribution will result in a 50 percent penalty on the amount not taken.

If there are multiple accounts, the IRA required minimum distributions can be taken entirely from one of the IRA accounts, as long as the calculation is based on the total balance of all IRAs. If there is money in a qualified plan, those distributions have to come out of that specific qualified plan. For example, if there is money sitting in multiple 401ks, they all have to be dealt with separately. This is another reason why many people prefer to consolidate all of their retirement investments into a single account. Trying to keep track of all the requirements and rules on multiple accounts can get confusing.

A Roth IRA provides great tax efficiency and flexibility because it has no required minimum distribution. The government has already received their taxes on the money, so they're not waiting on anything. Not only is there no minimum distribution on a Roth IRA, but your children can inherit it and they won't pay taxes on the distributions either.

ROTH IRAS AND ZERO-TAX YEARS

If you're a business owner, you might occasionally have a zero-tax year. Maybe you buy a lot of equipment, or perhaps you experience significant depreciation, and as a result, you wind up with a large deduction on your taxes that year. Even if you're not a business owner, you might have other deductions such as large healthcare expenses or charitable contributions. When that happens, it's a good idea to convert money into a Roth IRA, because the money won't be taxed that year—or at least, it will be taxed in a lower bracket. It's very advantageous to make large Roth conversions in low-tax or zero-tax years, so be ready to jump on the opportunity.

EMPLOYEE STOCK OWNERSHIP PLAN (ESOP)

An Employee Stock Ownership Plan is designed to invest in a sponsoring employer's stock. They're more common with employee-owned firms, because they give employees a strong sense of ownership in the company.

Some people get nervous about having a significant portion of their retirement plan invested in their company stock, but our experience has shown that ESOPs can be very promising for participants. We advise clients to make sure they understand the details of their specific ESOP plan.

In most cases, the stock is private, meaning it doesn't trade on the market. You can't track the share price daily as you can with publicly traded stocks. Often, privately held stocks are priced once per year by an outside firm that examines the metrics in the firm to determine the company value. In other cases, they are priced on a quarterly basis. Whatever the case, management is required to communicate this information to employees.

One of the dangers of an ESOP is that your investment is heavily weighted in the company's performance. Even if a company's stock has performed well, past performance doesn't guarantee future results. Fortunately, many of the ESOPs we've seen allow employees to diversify their holdings within the plan once they reach a certain age—typically around fifty—but each plan is different.

We've seen instances where an ESOP plan did so well that employees contributed nothing to their 401k. However, my advice is to maximize your 401k and not rely solely on an ESOP because an ESOP carries greater concentration risk. Be aware, there's usually a vesting schedule, meaning you have to be employed a certain amount of time before ESOP shares are awarded, but the same often goes for company contributions to a 401k.

Finally, as with an IRA or 401k, there are nuances involved with taking money out of an ESOP account at retirement. The harsh reality is that companies tend to prefer that *current* employees of the company be the primary beneficiaries of company shares rather than retired employees, so they create a select window in which liquidation of shares must occur once you leave the firm. It might be a year or two after you've left the firm. In some cases, you must liquidate shares almost immediately upon retirement. Also, understanding the timing of the next pricing is important. This all may play into your specific retirement date, because you will want to maximize your return.

MAXIMIZE COMPANY CONTRIBUTIONS TO YOUR 401K

If your company matches your contributions to a 401k, 403b, or similar plan, I strongly encourage you to take advantage of this. It's free money, and how often do we see free money in the world today? Understand what your company's policy is about matching contributions, and make the most of it.

Put as much into your 401k as you possibly can without compromising your lifestyle, even if your company will only match a certain amount. Start doing this early, so you're planting seeds for your retirement with pre-tax dollars as early as possible. At the very least, get the full company match on your 401k, but go beyond, if you can afford to do so.

CONSIDER YOUR TOOLS

The plans described in this chapter are the primary retirement tools available to you when planning for your retirement. Find out which tools your company offers, and make the most of your options.

Ideally, after maximizing your investments in at least some of these retirement accounts, once you are at or near retirement, you're going to have to create a spending plan and stick to it, so that's what we'll look at next.

Chapter Three

CREATE A SPENDING PLAN

If you're thinking about retirement planning, you're already ahead of the game. Roughly 90 percent of the people who come into my office have been saving and investing for years. The other 10 percent are people who have come into sudden money, such as from an inheritance or even lottery winnings. We've dealt with professional athletes and performers who received sudden large payments for work.

Those who have built their wealth slowly over the years tend to have more wisdom and discipline about money, while those who come into a sudden windfall often struggle to adjust. They haven't developed an attitude of deferred gratification toward money because they haven't had to, so learning to spend wisely can be difficult.

Sometimes, the clients I work with have taken a lump sum payout from a company pension fund or have received profit-sharing. Some have participated in the ESOP plans discussed earlier. In these situations, it is possible that the client hasn't saved any of their own money. The companies have handled and contributed to these respective accounts, so they haven't learned to save and invest over the long term. They have little experience dealing with market cycles, corrections, bear markets, and the emotions and discipline that go along with being a successful long-term investor.

I had a client almost twenty years ago who had money in a profit-sharing account the company had awarded him over time, but he had saved almost no money of his own. He had developed very little financial discipline, but I still tried to work with him, helping him diversify and create a spending plan.

Within six months, he had completely compromised the plan we came up with, spending more than a third of the money—money that was supposed to last for the rest of his life. He was only in his fifties, so he had many years ahead of him, but he'd sunk money into a dream home in the mountains, furnishing it with credit cards. Ultimately, he wound up in a situation where his assets were depleted well before they were supposed to have been.

Twenty years later, I'm a lot wiser, and I can see these situations coming from a mile away. At Keen Wealth Advisors, we do our best to advise people against making these kinds of rash spending decisions in their retirement, but you can't always change someone's nature. Whatever your situation, I strongly encourage you to be realistic and disciplined about the cost of retirement. It is *absolutely imperative* that you create a spending plan and stick with it.

Fortunately, most of the people I work with are prudent and willing to live within a spending plan. Notice that I say "spending plan" and not "budget." While they may seem to be the same thing, sometimes semantics make a difference. A "spending plan" is perceived as proactive and intentional, while the term "budget" may feel restrictive and cause people to avoid doing the work to get it right. Some clients come to us knowing exactly what they will be spending. In other cases, we work with them to nail it down. As you begin to think about your own spending plan for retirement, it might be helpful to know what you should include.

THE STARTING POINT

Often, when we begin discussing creating a spending plan for retirement, clients will say, "I have no idea what I'll need for retirement." Maybe you feel the same way.

As a starting point, I recommend taking a look at your current spending. Compare your monthly income to your monthly expenses. What is the trend? Is your consumer debt growing, or are you saving money? If you're making $7,000 a month after taxes, that tells me you most likely can live on $7,000 a month or less in retirement, which at least gives you a starting point.

Generally, you should be able to live on about two-thirds of your gross income from when you were working, because you will no longer have the same transportation costs, need for professional clothes, or other expenses related to a full-time career. You also will not be paying FICA taxes on retirement income, and you likely won't be saving anymore. It's important to figure this out up front, because you don't want to enter retirement expecting to live off $7,000 a month only to learn the hard way that you actually need $8,000 a month, or more. Are there expenses you aren't taking into consideration, such as Christmas or holiday shopping? Sometimes, we have clients who routinely help their children, grandchildren, or parents without considering it part of their expenses, so they are regularly spending more than they realize. You don't want to discover this the hard way after retirement.

Look at your financial records for the last year or two, and make sure you have a clear picture of what you bring in and what you spend each month. Figure out *exactly* what you're spending money on. In retirement, you will be able to remove all work-related expenses, but healthcare expenses will now kick in.

LIVING ON LESS OR LIVING ON MORE

Most of the people we work with have already been practicing delayed gratification and demonstrating restraint over the years. They've found a happy medium and lived comfortable lives, but they've saved money consistently and lived within their means. Once they reach retirement, they finally get to enjoy the fruits of their discipline.

It can be difficult to navigate the transition from saving money to now spending that money. For disciplined people, saving money has been part of who they are, so it can take time to get used to spending it instead. Some people are savers by nature, and they want to include savings as a retirement expense. Of course, when you save money during retirement, you are essentially just taking money from one pocket and putting it in another.

In the majority of cases, people choose to live on less once they've retired, and that's their choice to make. In a few cases some choose to live on substantially more, but their asset base has to sustain it. Whatever you decide, leave room for inflation, because costs always tend to go up, even if your income stays the same. From 1926 through

2018, the average annual inflation rate in the US was just under 3 percent.[2]

If you're going to live on more, ask yourself what you're going to be spending more money on. Maybe you have certain passions you want to pursue. If so, include that in your spending plan. For example, we have several clients who included a wine budget because they are passionate wine connoisseurs. In each case, they love to travel the world to experience different wines, and they maintain an impressive inventory at their homes. We made sure to include that in their spending plans.

Other clients might enjoy hunting, or shooting clay pigeons, or visiting exotic locations. Sometimes, they want to live in expensive retirement communities. I've met clients who, like me, are private pilots, which isn't a cheap hobby. I met another client who was into woodworking, and he needed to spend money on equipment and raw materials.

Maybe you have a hobby that you're hoping to splurge on throughout your retirement. That's perfectly fine. Just make sure to work it into your spending plan, so you know it's within your means. It's all too easy for costs associated with a personal passion to get out of control.

2 "U.S. Inflation Rate, $1 in 1926 to 2018," *CPI Inflation Calculator*, https://www.officialdata.org/1926-dollars-in-2018?amount=1, accessed April 8, 2019.

THE GO-GO, SLOW-GO, AND NO-GO YEARS

We call the first ten years of retirement the "go-go" years because many people are very active and spend way more money during those years than they do later on. Spending tends to drop off in the middle retirement years, which we call the "slow-go" years, when people might not be able to travel as much. Even if they still have money, and they've stuck to their plan, they tend to naturally moderate their activities.

Finally, in the "no-go" years, when people are typically in their late seventies and eighties and beyond, they're often spending much less money. They've given up most of their expensive hobbies, and they are content to relax at home.

There are exceptions, of course. We have clients in the "no-go" years who will pay for their whole family to go on vacation. One client took twenty-two family members on a Disney cruise at a cost of well over $100,000. However, it was an intentional decision that they made and planned for, so they had the money to do it without compromising their spending plan.

Finally, you must take into consideration that life throws curveballs. You can't prepare for everything, so you must be nimble and take some things as they come. Healthcare costs have risen at almost twice the rate of inflation, so it's important to take these into consideration in your spending plan. However, it's almost impossible to predict what your personal healthcare costs are going to be throughout your retirement, including long-term care such as assisted living or a nursing home.

Some people never end up needing any kind of long-term care, some need it only for a short period of time, but a select few will need it for many years. Knowing how to plan and budget for long-term healthcare needs can be difficult.

This is an adjustment that catches many people off guard. When you're working, your health insurance costs come out of your pay before you see the check, but now you will be paying for healthcare out of your bank account. Make sure you've considered the costs of Medicare and supplemental insurance. Bear in mind, medical insurance before age sixty-five can be as high as $2,000 a month for a couple. A good spending plan should take into account all of the different types of medical costs that could catch you off guard.

For more information on preparing for long-term care, check out our podcast episode "Long-Term Care and Your Financial Plan" at https://www.keenonretirement.com/long-term-care/.

HOW GRANULAR SHOULD IT BE?

In my experience, the more granular you can be in your spending plan, the easier it will be to stick with it. When you start planning for retirement, it's fine to have a general idea, but as you're gliding toward your retirement date, you need to get very specific. It's no longer a theory at this point.

I've met some people who were wizards at budgeting and working with available resources, but they still benefited from breaking down their spending into minute details. That way, when the time comes to take that trip you've been wanting to take, or to join that country club, or to buy that RV, you're ready for it. Even if it's a big expense, you've planned and prepared for it, so you've already given yourself permission to spend the money.

Most of the people we work with wind up with more money at the end of their life than they've ever had. That's fine, if that's what you want. However, I always want to make sure people enjoy the resources they've accrued for their retirement. If you create healthy parameters, then you don't have to feel guilty about spending your money, even splurging on your big-dream items.

A granular spending plan helps spouses get on the same page, and that is incredibly important, which is why at Keen Wealth Advisors, when we are dealing with a couple, we always make sure to meet with both spouses. If couples aren't on the same page with their spending and investing, it's a recipe for disaster. Getting granular with your spending plan gives you the perfect opportunity to talk through all of these issues with your spouse. This will be important when it comes to making financial decisions in the future.

WHO LIVES LONGER?

When planning for retirement, you will be making a lot of life decisions. It's important to bear in mind that women typically live longer than men—and plan accordingly.

My co-host and I were discussing this on the *Keen On Retirement* podcast the other day, and we pointed out something that many people don't realize. As it turns out, married men live longer than single men. That makes sense to most people. However, did you know married women live *shorter lives* than single women? My wife brought this to my attention, and since we like to tease each other in fun, we laughed about it.

"It's because we married women have to deal with all of your *issues*," she said. "It shortens our lives!"

While we had fun riffing on the subject on the podcast, life expectancy should play a role in your retirement planning. It's not always pleasant to think about, but it will be a significant factor at some point.

HOW MUCH SHOULD I SPEND EACH YEAR?

It's easier to accumulate $1 million or more than many people realize. If young people are prudent and start saving a decent amount of their paychecks consistently, they can easily have a million or multiple millions by retirement. When it comes to retirement, how much can you withdraw annually when you start spending those millions?

The age-old retirement rule says a reasonably safe withdrawal rate is 4 percent of your total nest egg per year. If you've accrued $1 million, that means you could spend $40,000 a year. However, if you look at US equity markets, they have generally produced a 10 percent rate of return over the last hundred years or so.[3] Small cap securities and international securities may generate even more than that. However, if you put money in the stock market, creating a diversified portfolio of stocks with a 10 percent a year return, that doesn't mean you should take out 10 percent a year. Of course, most folks will have a portion of their portfolios in fixed income investments as well, which will bring down the total return of the portfolio in exchange for providing some stability.

In the world of investing, it's often three steps forward, one step back. Never is it a straight line. While your equity

---

3 "S&P 500 Return Calculator, with Dividend Reinvestment: January 1919 – January 2019," DQYDJ, https://dqydj.com/sp-500-return-calculator/.

portfolio might average 10 percent over time, there will be times when the market takes a dramatic downturn. These downturns have always been temporary, but if you take out everything you've earned over time from your equities, when the market goes through its normal, cyclical, inevitable downturns, you will lock in the losses and most likely begin to fall behind on your spending plan. With a single year of bad decision-making, you can fall far enough behind that you never fully recover.

You might be tempted to invest your money more aggressively so you can spend more, but that can also be a recipe for disaster. We strongly dissuade clients from this kind of thinking. Four percent is typically a good starting place. Some prefer to start a little higher, since they intend to live a bit more exorbitantly during the early "go-go" years of retirement. That's fine. You might spend 6 percent per year during the first five years, when you have the energy and desire to be a lot more active, and then you can slow down to 4 percent or less once you start to spend more time at home. Just do this intentionally, so you don't spend down your money without meaning to.

Sometimes, retirees decide to postpone receiving their Social Security checks for a few years, although the longest you should postpone taking it is age seventy. We'll talk about the nuances of Social Security in a later chapter, but postponing it can allow people to take more than 4 percent for a certain period of time.

For example, a retiree might take more from their investments from age sixty-three to seventy, during which their per year withdrawal could be much higher than 4 percent. This wouldn't be sustainable indefinitely, but in this case, the retiree knows Social Security will kick in at a later date, at which time they can reduce the withdrawals from their investments.

SURPRISING EXPENSES

Some things will prove to be more expensive during retirement than most people expect. For example, it used to be commonly accepted that buying a house was a great investment, but in reality, a house can be a huge money drain. Windows need replacing, the AC goes out, tree branches fall and damage the roof. Insurance doesn't cover everything, and there are also utilities every month. Even if you've paid off the mortgage, you still have property taxes, insurance, and upkeep.

As a result, we're seeing a trend where more and more retirees are renting apartments or condos in communities where maintenance is provided. Reducing expenses is far more important than building equity during retirement, so it makes sense. Renting is a way of "controlling the controllable" in regard to upkeep, repairs, and regular maintenance. It can also reduce stress.

Earlier we mentioned Christmas and holiday expenses. As it turns out, this is one of the biggest surprise expenses for many retirees. During the holiday season, they buy presents for a spouse, children, and grandchildren, and when the credit card bill shows up in January, they are shocked to discover they spent $10,000 or more! It's a common problem, so be aware of it. Work this into your spending plan, especially if you have a large family or a lot of grandchildren. Get out ahead of the expense, rather than letting it take you by surprise.

It's not unlike the phenomenon I experience when I go to a nice restaurant. I order a bunch of delicious food without thinking about the calories. I'm just hungry. Before I know it, I've eaten over 1,500 calories in a single meal. These are the times where I'd rather not know the calories I'm consuming, but of course many restaurants now place the calories on the menu. Unfortunately, this is unsustainable.

When it comes to retirement planning, the idea is to create clear parameters and live within them. You don't want to be caught off guard or taken by surprise by making uninformed decisions. The purpose of a spending plan is to work out the details so you will know where you stand, no matter what curveballs life throws at you in the future. It is essential to a successful retirement, so start thinking through the fine points now.

Of course, to do that, you will have to figure out *when* you're going to retire. Let's investigate that question next.

Chapter Four

DETERMINE WHEN TO RETIRE

Earlier, I mentioned an engineer who determined his exact retirement date when he was still forty years from retiring. He knew when he wanted to retire, and he also knew approximately what his asset base would be when it happened.

I am honored to work with this gentleman and his wife, and I'm still astonished at how well he stuck to his plan. I'm a big proponent of planning and being intentional in life, but it takes an impressive amount of discipline to stick to a retirement plan for forty years. It's even more impressive that he came within six months of his goal.

I talked to another gentleman from the same company who was on the executive leadership team and worked in the finance department. He was forty when I first met with him, and he told me he wanted to retire at fifty. He was adamant about this, and when I probed for a purpose, I learned that his father had passed away at a relatively young age. This made the client determined to retire early enough that he would enjoy the next phase of his life in his early fifties.

He knew time was a precious commodity, and even though he could have had many more promising years in his career, he preferred to retire early and enjoy his life pursuing his passions and spending time with his wife. We created a plan to help him prepare, and he stuck with it. He hit his goal, retiring at age fifty, and I've had the joy of seeing him thrive in retirement for the past several years.

Both of these examples reveal what you can achieve if you plan and execute your retirement well. This is particularly important in the world of engineering. We work with a lot of engineers, and we see many firms go through dramatic cycles. One department can prosper while another department down the hall is letting people go. Because of the frequency of downsizing, many people are retiring sooner than they thought they would.

In any industry, however, a personal health problem or family tragedy can force someone to retire sooner than they intended.

THE BEST TIME TO RETIRE

Retirement literacy isn't taught in schools. Companies won't give retirement advice out of concern for liability. My firm is trying to fill in this education gap. I've taught a series of classes over the past twenty-plus years to educate people on many topics related to retirement, and there's a question I frequently ask, especially when I have new attendees:

"From a purely financial standpoint, when is the best time to retire?"

The most common answer is sixty-two, because that's the earliest you can receive Social Security. Others say sixty-five, because that's when you can receive Medicare. Some say fifty-nine-and-a-half, because that's the soonest you can start taking money out of an IRA without a penalty. Finally, a few will say fifty-five, because that's when you can take money directly from a retirement plan at work without a tax penalty.

Occasionally, someone will say, "From a purely financial standpoint, the best time to retire is *never*," and believe it or not, that's the correct answer.

From a financial standpoint, you can always work another year and save just a little more money. There's always a reason to justify putting off retirement—another year of saving and investing, another year of not spending.

I don't want to encourage anyone to retire before it's prudent, but I believe that when you have the resources to retire, you should consider doing so. There's a lot more to life than just saving and investing until your dying day.

There comes a crossover point—financially, mentally, and emotionally—when you know it's time to leave the saving phase of your life behind and start spending and enjoying your time. Sometimes that crossover point is crystal clear, and sometimes it isn't, but it generally comes at the point when you realize, "One more year of income isn't worth one more year of my life."

How valuable is your time with your family, your health, your passions, your hobbies? So many clients are fully committed to their work, and while that's admirable, that commitment starts to come at a heavy cost. They don't have time to exercise, sleep well, eat well, or relax. They can't settle down at night. When they take into consideration the time spent commuting, they spend ten to twelve hours or more every day working. It can be a constant, relentless rat race that never ends.

When is the right time to get off the proverbial work treadmill and on the real treadmill and start focusing on your health, well-being, and dignity as you enter into the next chapter of your life? When we talk to clients about this, we often find that they just want someone to tell them it's okay to begin thinking about themselves. That it is okay for them to stop working and start living on what they've accumulated. Some people make this decision by crunching numbers themselves, but it can be helpful to have the input of a financial advisor with years of experience, who has dealt with recessions and market corrections. That perspective can help you enter your retirement with confidence.

However, to put it succinctly: my goal is for you to retire when you can *afford* to do so, and to do it while you are still able to *enjoy* your retirement.

CAN YOU AFFORD TO RETIRE?

To determine if you can afford to retire, make sure you've completed the exercise from the previous chapter. Do you have a clear understanding of what you spend from month to month? That number will be the lever that makes your whole retirement plan work.

Now, consider the return you are currently getting from your investments and retirement accounts. You have to allocate your investments in such a way that they can pay for your lifestyle. For example, you most likely will never want your retirement portfolio to consist entirely of stocks, but you might have to increase your equity exposure in order to generate a little more return within reason. However, be careful not to take too many risks here, as there will likely be multiple market corrections and several bear markets during your retired life.

This may sound strange, but you also need to consider the date of your death. Obviously, if you live to be ninety-two, you're going to need quite a bit more money than if you only live to be eighty. I've had clients who have looked at the financial plan we put together and said, "You have me living until ninety-two. Can you just have me living until eighty-two? Then I would have enough money to retire today."

Of course, you can't and shouldn't try to orchestrate the date of your death, but if you know you have a health condition that shortens your life expectancy, or if you have a family history where no one lives past eighty, then you might take that into consideration when crunching the numbers. However, you must be careful pulling back the date of death simply to make your plan work. You want to be rational and reasonable. Don't create a plan that assumes you won't live past seventy just so the plan will say you can afford to retire sooner.

Taking all of these things into consideration, look at your spending and figure out how much money your retirement plan needs to produce. How much does your plan need to deposit into your checking account net of taxes each year? I know of married couples that receive $50,000 or more through Social Security alone, and they live comfortably on that amount. They might take the minimum distribution from their IRA when they turn seventy-and-a-half, but they are enjoying their lives even without it. If they have no debt, then they are able to travel and do other things they enjoy, so their plan works in perpetuity. For others it requires much more.

SET YOUR PARAMETERS

When you set the parameters for your retirement plan, you have to be realistic and not put a plan together that simply says what you want it to say. Occasionally, we will have clients who want to push the parameters beyond the practical. "You guys are telling me we would be okay with $5,000 a month," they might say, "but another firm said we could plan on spending $8,000 a month, so we're going with them."

I want people to maximize their standard of living in retirement, but I won't recommend that a client create parameters that are bound to compromise them. Be very careful not to fall into this trap. Don't latch onto an advisor who tells you what you want to hear. Make sure the numbers will work in real life. Don't be too conservative, but find a healthy balance that will allow you to be nimble going forward.

You don't have to become a Certified Financial Planner™ yourself in order to understand how the various inputs of your retirement plan work. A financial advisor can help fill in the gaps in your knowledge base. Just remember, there's no free lunch. You need a realistic plan that can meet your spending plan for the entirety of your retirement.

Chief among the decisions you will have to make is when to start taking Social Security. We find that many people scoff at Social Security, but if you and your spouse have both paid into the system, your monthly income from this one piece of your retirement plan could be substantial—in some cases over $5,000 a month. That creates a valid source of income for many people, and it's at least a great base to start from. The timing of Social Security will factor into the retirement date you choose, so let's take a look at how it will impact all of your retirement decisions.

Chapter Five

PLAN FOR SOCIAL SECURITY

We met with a client who had been widowed for several years by the time she was referred to us. As we looked at her financial situation, we realized she wasn't taking her Social Security widow's benefit. The widow's benefit was enacted in 1956, so it had been around for a long time. However, she wasn't aware of it, and at the time she was over sixty, struggling to get by.

She had gone down to the Social Security office and signed up for her own benefit without realizing that she could have taken her widow's benefit instead and let her own continue to accumulate until age seventy. She could have then switched to her own benefit at age seventy and had a much higher monthly income.

SOCIAL SECURITY BASICS

Will Social Security be here for the current generation of workers? Will it be here for future generations? Concerns about the solvency of the program are a frequent topic of conversation in the political arena.

To understand Social Security's future, it is helpful to understand its past. President Franklin D. Roosevelt signed the Social Security Act in 1935 as a direct response to the hardships brought on by the Great Depression. Social Security taxes were collected for the first time in 1937, with both workers and employers paying a part, as they do today. Back then, only 1 percent of the first $3,000 in wages was taxed. In 1939, Roosevelt signed legislation establishing benefits for dependents and survivors.

In 1937, when the first taxes were collected, life expectancy in the US was 58 years for men and 62.4 for women.[4] Since people couldn't take Social Security until they were sixty-five, it was a benefit that many wouldn't even get to enjoy. It certainly wasn't designed to pay out over a thirty-year retirement.

In 1965, Social Security payments for divorced wives were established, with payments for divorced husbands following in 1977. In 1972, President Nixon signed legislation authorizing cost-of-living adjustment for Social

4 http://www.demog.berkeley.edu/~andrew/1918/figure2.html.

Security, to be automatically applied each year. This was done because the economy was going through a period of hyper-inflation. Social Security disability payments were also established that year with the Supplemental Security Income (SSI) program, which is funded by general tax revenues instead of Social Security taxes. SSI was designed to provide income for low-income or no-income individuals with disabilities.

Social Security fell on hard times in the early 1980s, and for the first time, people began to worry that it would become insolvent. To address this fear, President Reagan signed legislation in 1983 that taxed benefits. Now, some of the money that was put in as a tax on income was taxed again when it was given to retirees.

It was an unusual change to the program. After all, Social Security is already paid out of FICA taxes withheld from both employers and employees. It's taxed income to begin with, so it makes sense that when you receive the benefit, the money would then be tax-free. Reagan's legislation made half of Social Security funds taxable, limiting it to the half put in by employers. That at least made it more palatable to the general population.

Unfortunately, this new tax didn't fix the system, so the government increased the amount of taxable income, with the percentage of taxable benefit placed on a sliding scale that can make as much as 85 percent of your Social Security taxable.

In 1982, still trying to protect the program, the minimum age for full retirement benefits was increased from sixty-five to sixty-seven. In 2000, President Clinton signed the Senior Citizens' Freedom to Work Act, eliminating the retirement earning test (RET) for people above full retirement age, a law that formerly prevented recipients of Social Security from working at the risk of losing their Social Security benefits.

The Social Security system continues to evolve to this day, so we can be certain that there will be additional adjustments in years to come. It is also likely that the full retirement age will be extended again at some point as life expectancy increases. Additionally, it is highly likely that the wage base at which FICA taxes are withheld will be increased, which in turn means that Social Security will almost certainly still be in place for the generation approaching retirement today.

HOW LONG SHOULD YOU WAIT?

When I sit down to discuss retirement with a new client, many of them initially scoff at the idea of Social Security being a significant part of their retirement. They haven't planned on it being there. There is a widespread belief that it will soon become insolvent, but, as we've said, that is almost certainly not the case.

Social Security can create a nice base, especially if two people who have paid into the system over the course of a lifetime are receiving it and living in the same household. As previously mentioned, it's not uncommon to see couples receiving over $5,000 per month just from Social Security combined in some cases. That income alone could feasibly support a family without any income from other sources.

As you begin to focus on your retirement planning, you can get a clear estimate on what your Social Security income will be at the Social Security Administration website (SSA.gov). At that point, you can think about the best way to apply various options that are available to you.

The number-one question we get about Social Security is, "When should I start taking it?" We've seen people take Social Security as soon as they possibly can, thinking, "I want to get my fair share before it goes away." Others ask, "Should I delay taking Social Security so the amount I receive is more?" Of course, the answer depends on your other retirement accounts, as well as your personal retirement plan.

We know that Social Security increases approximately

8 percent every year it is delayed, but if you choose to delay it until later, you have to replace that income from your investments or some other source. Do you have an asset base you can live on while you allow Social Security to increase in value? The longer you wait, the more your monthly checks will be. Bear in mind, it will take time for those higher checks to make up for the months when you were receiving nothing from Social Security. It typically takes at least twelve years to make up the difference.

If you have the resources to allow Social Security to keep growing until you reach age seventy, then you have some decisions to make. There is no benefit for waiting past seventy. At this point, you will receive the highest amount that Social Security pays, so now your objective will be to live as long as possible to maximize your return.

If you don't have the resources to wait, then you don't have a choice. That's okay. There's nothing wrong with taking Social Security as soon as you can, if that's what you need to do. However, there are other considerations that people often miss.

SOCIAL SECURITY GUIDE

For a simple guide to help you make Social Security decisions, check out the *Keen On Retirement* podcast episode "The Pros and Cons of Taking Social Security Earlier or Later" at https://www.keenonretirement.com/taking-social-security/. You can also learn more about discount rates for taking Social Security early.

OTHER SOCIAL SECURITY CONSIDERATIONS

With a good portion of the couples we've worked with, one spouse worked full-time to earn their entire income while the other stayed at home. When the spouse who worked passes away, often the one who was a homemaker doesn't realize they are eligible for Social Security. They think, "I didn't pay into the system, so I can't get anything out of it." This is simply not true.

Every spouse can receive *either* their own benefit based on what they've paid into the system *or* half of the working spouse's benefit. They will receive the higher of the two, even if they never paid a dime in FICA tax. If your spouse paid the minimum of forty quarters to qualify for Social Security, then you can receive half their benefit. Even when your working spouse is still alive, you can receive half their benefit while they continue to receive their own full benefit. When most people learn this, it's a pleasant surprise, because it's not common knowledge.

When your spouse passes away, you will receive the higher of your two Social Security benefits. If you were a homemaker receiving half your spouse's benefit while they received their full benefit, then the smaller of the two will stop when your spouse passes away.

Depending on your situation, this may be a guiding factor for when you decide to start taking your Social Security benefit. Depending on the other assets in your portfolio, it might make sense to let the spouse with the higher Social Security benefit allow theirs to grow as long as possible so that when they are gone, the other spouse will receive a higher payout. It could be considered a lifetime pension for the surviving spouse.

The days of company pensions have largely come to an end, but Social Security is the closest thing most retirees have to a pension. In operation, it is very similar, and it is sure to play an important role in your retirement plans. Therefore, it is important to educate yourself on the program as you prepare for your future.

SOCIAL SECURITY MISTAKES

Mistake 1: Earnings Limit: Many people don't know about Social Security earnings limits. If you retire before full retirement age, and you decide to start working during your retirement, you can only earn a certain amount of money before your benefits are penalized. The earnings limit is adjusted for inflation each year, but as of 2019, it stands at approximately $17,640 a year. For every two dollars you earn over the limit, you lose a dollar of Social Security.

People think they can be fully employed during their retirement while still collecting Social Security benefits with no penalty, so they're caught off guard when they are informed that they've made too much money and have to repay some benefits.

Once you hit full retirement age, you can earn as much as you want without incurring penalties. The purpose of the earnings limit, after all, isn't to penalize retirees for working, but to encourage them not to take Social Security early if they're still going to work. Unfortunately, few people are aware of this, so they learn about the earnings limit the hard way. This is why it's so important to be fully educated about your retirement options. You don't want to be penalized and discover it's too late to correct the problem.

Mistake 2: Turning Off Social Security: Occasionally, I speak to people who are under the assumption that they can start and stop Social Security benefits whenever they want. The truth is, you can only turn off your benefits within twelve months of filing, so if you change your mind, you'd better do so early. Also, you only get one shot. Of course, if you repay all of your benefits, your Social Security account will reset as if you'd never claimed, but after the initial twelve months, you can't simply change your mind. In the past, there was a bit more flexibility in this regard, but the rules have become more restrictive in recent years.

Mistake 3: Spousal Benefits: As discussed earlier, many people are unaware that Social Security offers spousal benefits. If you coordinate when claiming your Social Security benefits, you and your spouse can often receive more than if you make independent decisions. You might be able to claim a spousal benefit while letting your own benefit continue to grow. It's an option that is worth investigating.

Mistake 4: Underestimating Survivor Benefits: Similarly, widows and widowers often fail to take full advantage of potential survivor benefits. They might not even know this is an option, but it can play an important role in your long-term retirement plans.

Mistake 5: Taxes: The taxation of Social Security income is unclear to many people. Essentially, when you receive money from Social Security, somewhere between 0 and 85 percent of that income will be considered taxable. If Social Security is your *only* source of income, then none of it is taxable. However, as other sources of income increase, more of it will become taxable, up to a maximum of 85 percent. Because of this, it's important to think carefully about which retirement accounts to draw from and in which order. If done right, you can minimize your Social Security tax, or at least stay in a lower tax bracket.

Mistake 6: Running Out of Money: Social Security ensures you will *never* completely run out of income, no matter what happens to the rest of your retirement accounts. Even if you have a few bad years in a row with your investments, even if you lose *everything else*, Social Security income will continue to the end of your life. Take this into consideration when making retirement decisions.

Chapter Six

OPTIMIZE YOUR TAXES

We had a client who was a successful business owner with a large amount of income and many investments. However, because of the nuances of business tax law, particularly the depreciation related to capital expenditures, he experienced a very large loss one year that carried over to his tax return. This gave him the opportunity to convert $300,000 from his traditional IRA into a Roth IRA with no taxes, but only if he did it the same year he experienced the loss. Although money is normally taxed when it's converted into a Roth IRA, in that particular year, he would have simply been offsetting the loss on his tax return.

We reached out to the client repeatedly in order to remind him about this opportunity, but he was so busy at his business that he missed the year-end deadline. We simply needed him to sign and return a few simple documents to effect the conversion, but he procrastinated. The $300,000 remained in his traditional IRA account, where it will ultimately be taxed when he withdraws it—a tragic loss he could have avoided with a Roth IRA conversion that year.

A Roth IRA conversion has to happen by December 31 of the year for which you're filing taxes. You can't wait until the tax filing deadline the following April. This is another reason why proactive tax planning is so very important.

Normally, the government loves when a Roth IRA conversion is made, because income tax is paid on the money in the year the conversion is made. Working people with a high income often avoid making these conversions because they don't want to pay more taxes. However, if you have an unusual year like the one described above, you can make a Roth IRA conversion without owing taxes. You should jump on it, but that requires paying attention and being proactive about your planning.

Another client of ours paid $300,000 to move into a nice retirement community, which allowed him to live independently and with dignity. Skilled nursing was available, paid for by the initial cost plus monthly fees. This is a common scenario in the nicer retirement communities across the country.

When we evaluated his contract, we realized that nearly half of the $300,000 he'd paid up front was considered qualified healthcare expenses, meaning he could itemize his income taxes that year and get a six-figure deduction. By discovering this in advance, we were able to recommend that the client convert six-figures from their traditional IRA to a Roth IRA that year. It was a narrow window of opportunity, but we caught it in time.

If we hadn't noticed this until tax season, it would have been too late. The December 31 deadline would already have passed. This is why it's so important to be proactive about your taxes.

TAX DECISIONS FOR RETIREMENT

In most cases, you will pay fewer taxes during retirement than you did in your working life, but this isn't always the case. It's important to understand the exceptions. One of the biggest tax decisions you will have to make in retirement has to do with qualified retirement plans, which are, in most cases, pretax savings. As you put money into a qualified plan over the years, you receive a tax deduction in the year those contributions are made. Money in those accounts grows tax-deferred, but once you start making withdrawals, taxes will be due. As we mentioned, Roth IRAs are a rare exception.

If you have a qualified retirement plan from your employer, you will have to decide whether to leave the money in the employer's plan or cut ties with your employer and shift the money into an IRA. At a bare minimum, you want to avoid triggering income taxes on the money you move out of your qualified plan at retirement. If you decide to transfer your assets out of a qualified plan into a self-directed IRA, make sure that the pretax money going into the IRA is going directly to the custodian of the IRA. Never take constructive receipt of the assets when making the transfer, or you will trigger a tax and an unexpected withholding and possibly a penalty.

Of course, if there are after-tax dollars in the plan, that portion is returned with no taxes due, so you want to keep that money separate. The after-tax contributions to a qualified plan can be rolled into a Roth IRA account and grow tax-free forever. This opportunity will most likely make sense. Before you make a transaction like this, I highly recommend you meet with a retirement planning specialist. Have them on the conference call with you to your qualified plan provider to guide and direct you through the transaction.

TAX BRACKETS AND ROTH IRA CONVERSIONS

Many people are confused about tax brackets. They believe that if they enter a higher tax bracket by one dollar, then their entire income will be taxed at a higher rate, and this belief has led some people to think it's a bad idea to make more money. The brackets don't work that way. If you slip into a higher tax bracket by one dollar, only the money over the threshold gets taxed at the higher level, not your entire income. On our website, KeenOnRetirement.com, you can find a list of current tax brackets to see where you stand.

Paying an effective rate of under 20 percent in total taxes isn't bad, but when retirees are paying over 20, even 30, percent or more, that's when it can start to hurt. We've had many clients who had very little taxable income other than Social Security and, because of deductions or simply spending from their after-tax accounts, were able to stay in a lower tax bracket. In that situation, it is smart to make a Roth IRA conversion. In fact, it's smart to make a Roth IRA conversion in any low tax year, at least up to the limit of the two lowest tax brackets, and maybe more.

This requires keeping an eye on your finances, assessing your tax situation mid-year so you can make a transfer into a Roth IRA by the deadline. Remember, you can't wait until taxes are due. The deadline for Roth IRA conversions is always December 31 of the previous calendar year.

REQUIRED MINIMUM DISTRIBUTIONS

At age seventy-and-a-half, the government will force you to take minimum distributions from your retirement accounts based on your life expectancy. The money that is forced out of your retirement account is taxable, so you have a window of opportunity to prepare for it. There is only one way to get out of paying taxes on minimum required distributions, and that is donating to charity. If you are already donating to a charity or would like to start, you should consider making qualified charitable donations (QCDs) from your required minimum distributions.

The amount you are required to take increases the longer you live. To give you an example of what to expect, a required minimum distribution on $1 million will be around $36,500—or 3.65 percent—a year. Since it's based on life expectancy, once you reach age ninety, you will be required to take closer to 10 percent a year. If you make it to age 115, you will be required to take 50 percent each year.

To reiterate, the longer you live, the more of a percentage the government will require you to take out of your IRA each year and pay taxes on. You can't convert required minimum distributions into a Roth IRA. In many cases, when our clients don't need the money, they shift it over to a taxable investment account, but the taxes still have to be paid.

INHERITED IRAS

If your kids are going to inherit your IRA, they need to understand what to expect. If your child inherits an IRA with $2 million in it, and they decide to take all of the money out in one year, they will suddenly find themselves in the highest income tax bracket. Nearly half of the money will vanish during tax season.

There's a way around this. It's called the *stretch provision*, and it extends the tax-deferred status of an inherited IRA when it is passed to your children or other non-spouse beneficiaries. For younger beneficiaries, these resources can remain and even make up part of their own retirement income. Instead of taking all the money out and paying a massive amount of taxes on it, they can take regular smaller distributions. The minimum distribution requirement still applies.

Because of the stretch provision, an IRA that you set up for yourself can continue to grow tax-deferred into your child's retirement long after you're gone. Although, they must abide by the minimum distribution rules, which can be tricky. If it's a Roth IRA, the money is tax-free when they inherit it, and they will *never* owe taxes on it. That makes a Roth IRA a wonderful inheritance. Please reference the *Keen On Retirement* podcast episode "Making the Right Choice When Inheriting an IRA" for a thorough explanation of inheriting these types of assets, at https://www.keenonretirement.com/inherited-ira/.

TAX DEDUCTIONS

As a result of the Tax Cuts and Jobs Act of 2017, it is estimated that over 90 percent of the people who file will take the standard deduction. The standard deduction has increased so much that there is no benefit for most people in itemizing their deductions.

The most common deductions include mortgage interest, qualified healthcare expenses, state and local taxes, and charitable giving. If you're self-employed, there are other business-related deductions you can take as well. However, when most people add up their total deductions from these major categories, they won't surpass the standard deduction. If you're an exception, then you should certainly itemize, though the standard deduction makes filing much easier. Even if you expect to take the standard deduction, you should track your expenses throughout the year so you can make sure that itemizing isn't advantageous for you.

In the tax reform bill of 2017, personal exemptions were eliminated. Some clients we meet with don't realize this. You can't claim yourself, your kids, or your spouse. Divorced couples no longer have to argue about who's going to claim the children. There are *no* personal exemptions. They've all been eliminated, though the child tax credit did increase, so as not to hit families. Remember, a tax credit is always worth more than a tax deduction.

TAX CODE CHANGES

For more information on the nuances of the most recent tax code changes, we have created a helpful webinar at https://www.keenonretirement.com/webinar-new-tax-bill/.

CHARITABLE DONATIONS

Most people give to charity because they want to make a difference, not because they're looking for a tax deduction. However, you earn the deduction, and you might as well make use of it. Of course, if you take the standard deduction, as most people will, you may not see an additional tax benefit for your giving.

Hopefully, this doesn't discourage people from making charitable contributions. One strategy is to cluster your charitable giving all in one year so the total you give surpasses the standard deduction. You can achieve this by only giving every other year, or every third year, depending on how much you donate.

Another popular method is a *donor-advised fund*, which

allows people to make charitable contributions and receive an immediate tax deduction. You put multiple years' worth of donations into the fund, take the deductions all in that year, and then you can decide how, where, and when to disburse the money over the years to come.

Charitable giving is also a good way to avoid paying taxes on required minimum distributions. A qualified charitable distribution (QCD) allows you to take money directly from the minimum distribution and send it to a 501c3 charity of your choice. You can even take the standard deduction while excluding the charitable distribution from your taxable income. If you're over seventy-and-a-half, receiving minimum distributions, and making donations to charity, you should consider QCDs. Remember, the money has to come directly from your IRA to the charity, and this rule does not apply to 401k accounts. I would highly recommend talking to your financial or tax advisor to ensure you get this right.

For a thorough discussion on charitable giving, listen to the *Keen On Retirement* podcast episode "3 Key Ways to Maximize the Impact of Your Charitable Giving" at https://www.keenonretirement.com/giving/.

ENTERING RETIREMENT DEBT-FREE

We find that many clients want to enter retirement debt-

COMMON TAX RETURN MISTAKES

I've put together a list of common tax mistakes from our own experiences and the IRS website (IRS.gov). These are things to watch out for when filing.

Mistake 1: A Missing or Wrong Social Security Number. Though it seems like a small thing, this is a common mistake that can cause major delays in the processing of your tax return. Always double- or triple-check to make sure your Social Security number is correct.

Mistake 2: Failing to Include All Sources of Income. Are there any sources of income, no matter how small, that you've overlooked? Even a small amount of income on a 1099 needs to be included, or you could wind up paying penalties.

Mistake 3: Math Errors. With all of the free online tax calculators that are available these days, you might think math errors are a thing of the past. However, many people still do the math by hand. Even when they use online tools, a mistake can be made if a number is entered incorrectly. When the math is wrong, it can cause problems that slow down the process.

Mistake 4: Claiming the Wrong Amount of Credits or Deductions. This is actually the biggest mistake that tax filers make. They claim either too many or too few deductions. Every year, millions of Americans attempt to claim credits that they aren't eligible for. Illegal deductions are construed as tax evasion by the IRS, opening you up for an audit.

Mistake 5: Forgetting to Sign and Date Your Return. This mistake is far more common than people realize. It seems like a simple thing, but it happens all the time.

Mistake 6: Failing to File. Maybe life is just too hectic. Maybe you're afraid of how much you'll owe. Maybe you just forgot. Whatever the case, failing to file your taxes will result in additional costs, interest, and penalties. If you need more time, you can request an extension in advance, but never miss the April 15 deadline without working it out with the IRS first.

Mistake 7: Forgetting to Include Your Payment. If you walk carefully through every step of preparing and filing your taxes, avoiding all of the previous mistakes, but then you don't include payment for taxes owed, the process has to start all over again. If you need to set up payments with the IRS because you owe more than you can pay, fill out the appropriate paperwork and file it along with your tax return.

free, and since their mortgage is likely their biggest piece of debt, they'll often try to make a large withdrawal from their IRA in order to pay off the home loan. We strongly recommend that you walk through the tax ramifications of making a large IRA withdrawal before you do this, especially if your home loan has a fixed rate. I believe it's smarter to pay off a fixed-rate mortgage over a number of years if your only source of funds is a pre-tax IRA. Making a large IRA withdrawal might put you in a higher tax bracket that year.

WHO CAN HELP PREPARE YOUR TAXES?

Many mistake tax preparation for tax planning. In my opinion, most tax professionals aren't thinking about your investments or your overall plan when they help prepare your taxes. They are simply reporting history. This is not a criticism; they are doing what they are hired to do. However, a good financial advisor with a proactive approach to tax planning, working alongside a CPA, can help you stay on top of all the complexities of preparing your taxes, particularly as it affects your retirement plan.

We've barely scratched the surface on the subject of income taxes. There is so much more to consider, and so many nuances that can impact you—positively or negatively. You can find more information at our *Keen On Retirement* website. Check out the following podcast episodes: https://www.keenonretirement.com/taxes-in-retirement/ and https://www.keenonretirement.com/year-end-tax-planning/.

Tax planning isn't just about you. Your heirs will have to deal with your will, trust, and, potentially, estate taxes. It's important to educate yourself so you can prepare your children or grandchildren. Ideally, you want to get your documents in order to make things as efficient as possible. Let's take a closer look.

Chapter Seven

PREPARING YOUR WILL AND TRUST

Several years ago, we received an interesting phone call. A gentleman had inherited a large amount of money that he hadn't expected. Normally, you wouldn't expect this to cause distress, but he was frantic. His ex-wife of thirty-five years had passed away the prior year, leaving him with a substantial inheritance from a life insurance policy.

After discussing it with numerous parties including his attorney, he realized this was most likely a mistake. His ex-wife had almost certainly forgotten to change the beneficiary on her policy when she got remarried, even though she was married to her new husband for thirty years until her death.

As you can imagine, the new spouse was furious and

insisted the proceeds be given to him. Our client was in a quandary. He didn't need the money, and he didn't want to be greedy, but he wasn't sure what to do. Complicating the matter, our client had children with his ex-wife, but the current spouse also had children with her.

Ultimately, and after much stress and contemplation, he decided not to take possession of the money himself. He put it into a trust and set it up for the children of both marriages.

THE IMPORTANCE OF ESTATE PLANNING

This story is just one example of how missing a simple beneficiary change can completely change the trajectory of someone's legacy after they pass away. Estate planning is how you take control of your property while you're alive, so you can make sure your money goes where you want, and to whom you want, when you're gone.

If you die without an estate plan—which is called *dying intestate*—state laws will determine how your assets are divvied up, and it may well not be how you prefer. We saw a dramatic example of this when the superstar singer Prince died. He had no will, so when he passed away, the courts got to decide how to split up and distribute his multimillion-dollar estate. It became a big public mess that has dragged on for years, involving numerous siblings and half-siblings.

Most people think of estate planning as simply an attempt to avoid estate taxes. When I began working in this industry in the early 1990s, a single person could only pass $600,000 in assets to their heirs' estate tax-free. Anything over that amount was taxed at approximately a 50 percent rate. For some people, these high estate taxes were brutal. Imagine a family farm worth several million dollars. When the owners passed away, the next generation who inherited the farm were required to pay 50 percent of anything over $600,000. This proved devastating, and many family farms and businesses were lost or sold on the cheap simply due to the estate tax burden.

Since then, the amount that can be passed without incurring estate taxes has been increased to over $11 million per person. While that is a much better situation, it doesn't mean you shouldn't have an estate plan, including a will and possibly a trust in place. Remember, this is about more than simply trying to avoid paying taxes. It's about *taking control of your property* while you're still alive, *taking care of your affairs and loved ones* if you become disabled, and giving what you have to *whomever you choose* when you're gone.

It's also about maintaining privacy and avoiding probate, which incurs additional costs. Most Americans won't go over the estate tax threshold, so only a select few will pay estate taxes under current law. The law could change, of course, but even if it doesn't, without establishing a will or living trust, the courts determine what happens to your assets. When the courts get involved, fees start to accrue—fees that are left to your heirs.

WILL VS. TRUST VS. POWER OF ATTORNEY

So what's the difference between a will and a trust? A will is a document that tells the courts what you want them to do with your assets. While this is a legitimate process, your estate still has to go through a probate court. All you're doing with a will is advising the probate court on how to distribute your assets, and since your estate goes through court, everything becomes public and fees are incurred. While a simple will is better than nothing, it isn't ideal.

The type of trust we most often deal with is called a *revocable living trust*. "Revocable" means that as the grantor, you can change it at any time while you're still alive. With a trust, you re-title your assets in the name of the trust, which guides and directs a trustee that you name ahead of time about what to do with your assets upon your death or if you become incapacitated. If you become unable to handle your own affairs, a trust provides direction in your absence.

A trust can also be *irrevocable*, which can be confusing

because the name suggests that once you set it up, no one will be able to change it—not even you. However, in certain circumstances, these kinds of trusts *can* be terminated. You should know going in that it will require following state laws, the cooperation of beneficiaries and trustees, and possibly a petition to the court to dissolve. Irrevocable trusts provide a greater degree of security for your assets—particularly against creditors—but they are more complex and have a higher tax rate. For most people, a revocable living trust accomplishes everything they need for their basic estate plan.

It's also important to have a *living will*, which tells people what should happen if you're too ill to make your own decisions, particularly in regard to resuscitation and life support. It allows you to give someone you trust the ability to make healthcare decisions for you. A power of attorney document also allows someone you select to make financial decisions on your behalf while you are living.

One problem we've seen is that people will give someone an active power of attorney and then forget about it. Later, their relationship preferences change—possibly from a divorce or other life circumstance—but they don't change the power of attorney document. For this reason, we recommend revisiting your estate planning regularly. You can also set up what's called a *springing* power of attorney, which only goes into effect when several doctors sign a document stating that you are incapacitated.

When you're working on your will or trust, don't worry about trying to account for every single thing that could possibly happen over your lifetime. While it is important to be thorough, some people put off drafting a will or trust because they don't think they can draft a perfect document that will handle every situation that might come up in the next twenty or thirty years and beyond. In reality, you only need to think about the next three to five years. Beyond that, life is going to happen. The power in this process comes from making changes to your documents as you have grandchildren, as people get married or divorced, and as things evolve. Adjustments are inevitable, and when a big life event happens, you can adjust accordingly. Just don't forget.

I always encourage clients to use a lawyer who specializes in estate plans rather than a generalist. While it may cost a few thousand dollars to set up your plan, you will be able to put your head on your pillow every night knowing that your assets are taken care of—that's priceless.

OUT-OF-DATE DOCUMENTS

We see clients all the time who made estate plans ten to twenty years ago or longer that are now woefully out of date. Remember, limit your thinking to the next three to five years, because life happens. Always check in with your financial advisor and estate planning attorney anytime a major life event happens, so you can update your documents if necessary.

We also have clients who have "updated" their will or trust on their own by scribbling notes on it, or adding yellow sticky notes, and initialing their changes. In most cases, this won't hold up in court. This kind of change will be easy to challenge, so we strongly encourage people to see an attorney when making changes, and to discuss it with a financial advisor during an annual review meeting.

Remember, your assets must be domiciled by the trust. This is not hard to do. If you own your home, you have to go down to the courthouse and put your house in the trust. If you open any new accounts, put them in the name of the trust. Update your retirement accounts and life insurance beneficiary designations to the name of the trust as counseled by your attorney. It's simple to make these updates, and no taxes are due. Practically speaking, nothing changes for you; your accounts are put in the name of the trust and your beneficiary designations are correct. If you fail to do this, the trust is essentially worthless because nothing has been directed into the trust.

REVIEW YOUR BENEFICIARIES

You should check with a financial advisor to confirm the beneficiaries of your accounts. It is common to make a spouse the primary beneficiary of an IRA, with the trust as contingent. Sometimes, a client will ask if the trust should own their IRA. The problem with this is that it requires taking money out of the IRA now to put it in the trust, and we would not recommend that. Remember, if it's a traditional IRA, that money is taxable when you withdraw it.

If you want, you can make the trust the beneficiary of the IRA, but we wouldn't technically put the IRA in the trust. This can sound very confusing, and it is. Every person's situation is different and requires discernment when establishing beneficiaries. Following the advice of solid legal counsel with the help of your financial advisor is imperative.

Anytime you open a new account, revisit your beneficiaries and make sure they aren't out of date. Remember, a beneficiary designation on an IRA, annuity, or life insurance policy will trump what your will or trust says, so make sure all of your designations are correct.

LEAVING MONEY TO ONE CHILD

Here's a scenario that we see from time to time. A client

has three adult children. The oldest child has their act together, the youngest child doesn't have their act together, and the middle child is somewhere in between the extremes. The client decides to leave all of their assets to the oldest child, hoping that they will then distribute the assets equally among the other siblings.

This is a terrible idea that can create severe tax ramifications for the oldest child. If one child inherits all of the money, they also inherit all of the tax obligations on that money. While estate taxes aren't as bad as they used to be, there is still income tax to worry about. They will owe money on traditional IRAs, annuities, and other assets. Even if they divide the money with their siblings, that one child gets all of the legal obligation to pay the taxes.

We've seen these situations create endless family squabbles. In fact, they can tear families apart. By giving everything to one child and trusting them to divide it for you, you are opening a can of worms. We strongly discourage it.

JOINT TENANCY

Another problem occurs when clients put their assets in joint tenancy with a child. This seems to make sense. If both the parent and child already own the assets, then it will be a simple thing for the child to take over those assets when the parent passes away. The problem is, those assets become subject to the child's creditors while the parent is still alive.

Also, the child can take the assets away at any time, even when the parent is still alive, because they've been given ownership. For example, a client will often create a joint bank account with a child, thinking, "This ensures that they can handle my money when I'm gone." However, by putting your child's name on your bank account, they can technically access the money at any time. It's their money now. Sadly, we've seen parents taken advantage of by children they trusted in these kinds of situations.

Yet another downside to joint tenancy is the loss of part of the "step-up in basis." A step-up in basis is the adjustment of the value of an appreciated asset for tax purposes upon inheritance, determined to be the value of the asset at the date of death of the original owner. When an asset is passed on to a beneficiary, its value is typically more than when the original owner purchased it. The asset receives a step-up in basis so that the beneficiary's capital gains tax is minimized.

For example, an investor purchasing shares at $10 and leaving them to an heir when the shares are $100 means the shares receive a step-up in basis, making the cost basis for the shares the current market price of $100. Any capital gains tax paid in the future will be based on the $100 cost basis, not on the original purchase price of $10. This is a very nice feature of the current tax law.

If you name your would-be beneficiary as a joint tenant before you pass away, they will lose the step-up in basis on half of the asset, and their cost basis would be $10 on that half and not $100. This applies to real estate and other assets as well.

FILE EVERYTHING

Finally, when it comes to estate planning, make sure to collect and file all of your important information, including bank records, insurance, and investment accounts, copies of your personal identification, property deeds, vehicle titles—everything! Gather all of these documents, scan them to make digital copies, and store them in a lockbox. Put the originals all in the same place, and make sure that at least your executor or trustee knows where to find them.

Make sure the passwords to your email addresses and social media accounts are written down and included with this paperwork. People rarely print photographs or write personal letters these days. All of those things are now on our social media accounts. If you have photo albums on Facebook, Instagram, or a Google account, they will be priceless to your heirs, so make sure your heirs can access them when you're gone.

PART TWO

BUILD THE ENGINE

Chapter Eight

CREATE THE ENGINE OF THE PLAN

Thus far, we've talked about planning your retirement life and creating a spending plan. We've discussed taxes, Social Security, wills, and trusts, but we haven't talked about the investments that are going to make your retirement possible. Your investments are the engine of your financial plan, and you have to make wise investment decisions to get and keep the engine running. You can't take this part for granted or hope it works out.

There are countless marketers and promoters with an endless array of investment vehicles, but many of their products won't provide the return you expect or need for your financial plan. Some of them may well be riddled with very high commissions, hidden costs, and risks that aren't clearly explained, if at all.

A client was referred to us, and when we looked at his portfolio, we discovered that most of his assets were tied up in twelve different non-traded real estate investment trusts (REITs), each of which had been sold to him with the promise of a high return and no downside. We attempted to help him get a handle on his situation, but in the end, he was only able to retrieve about half of his initial investment. Several of the investments had already gone completely off the radar, and two-thirds of them remained illiquid past their promised dates of liquidity.

These types of investments can destroy someone's retirement, but the client simply hadn't realized what he was getting into. The salespeople who pushed these particular non-traded REITs hadn't warned him about their risk. Knowing who to trust is one of the biggest challenges for people navigating toward retirement, and the world of investing is fraught with peril.

WHO CAN YOU TRUST?

Every day in the United States, approximately ten thousand people enter retirement.[5] That number is bandied about quite a bit, and it has marketers salivating. There are so many institutions marketing products to retirees,

---

5 John Landau, "Health-care dilemma: 10,000 boomers retiring each day," *CNBC*, October 3, 2017, https://www.cnbc.com/2017/10/03/health-care-dilemma-10000-boomers-retiring-each-day.html.

and so much information bombarding people, that it can be very difficult to separate the real news from the noise.

Most people get their information from the media, but the media's constant fearmongering is the enemy of long-term investing. It can scare you and cause you to compromise your plan by making knee-jerk reactions because of some report that claims the sky is falling.

We all remember the night Donald Trump won the presidential election. To many, it was a surprise, and the markets went into freefall that night. However, it was actually the *futures* market, which, in part, deals with what might happen when the *real* equity market opens the following morning. By the time the market opened, it was up nicely, but not before we saw a thousand points of downside volatility in the futures market overnight and the media jumped all over it. This type of scenario can provoke people to have emotional reactions.

As if market volatility dramatized by the media wasn't enough, people approaching retirement are constantly targeted with mailings. Maybe you've already started to receive them—seminar invitations that arrive in your mailbox promise free steak dinners at nice local restaurants in exchange for a presentation about a magic investment. What is the magic investment? Something that captures all of the upside of the equity markets with none of the downside, of course! Often, that means an equity index annuity pitch may be coming. It often sounds too good to be true, and typically is, especially the way they are commonly presented.

It's easy to trust people in nice suits, especially when they give you free steak dinners. They make it all sound so easy. Sadly, we've seen these kinds of assets have a net seven-figure *negative* impact on a client's portfolio over the course of their lives.

Some of these sales-pitch seminars are positioned as educational courses that will enlighten people about their retirement options, but there's always a sales pitch before the "educators" leave the room. While I encourage folks to go out and learn as much as possible about their options, we strongly encourage people to do their homework before attending any of these informational sessions or seminars. Never sign on the dotted line or commit to anything until you've had a fiduciary financial advisor take a look at the opportunity. At the very least, spend some time thinking very carefully about any investment opportunity before you buy the pitch.

THREE WAYS TO HOLD MONEY

As I've taught classes over the past twenty-plus years, I've found that people of all ages and experience levels appreciate it when I lay things out simply. I do this with professional engineers as much as I do when speaking to grade school kids about financial literacy.

EQUITY INDEX ANNUITIES

Equity index annuities are often promoted with the promise that clients can participate in the upside of the stock market with no downside. However, they typically deliver returns that are comparable to a treasury bond or short-term CD—that is to say, quite low. Often, they tie your money up for as long as fifteen years, with heavy penalties if you try to get out early.

In essence, with an index annuity, you are giving money to an insurance company, which provides some modest, formulaic return. It's true, in most cases, there's no participation in the downside of the market. However, the upside will most likely be small at best, and people who dump a bunch of money into these annuities are often shocked at how little they get in return.

The salesperson can receive 10 percent commission to sell these products, so they naturally want to push for a big investment. If they can get a client to put $1 million into an index annuity, they walk away with $100,000—with no incentive to service the account or provide any counsel to the investor until they are out of the surrender charge period and able to do it all over again.

In certain cases, these products can be appropriate, but only if they are explained accurately and understood by the investor. In many instances, we have seen that the salespeople don't fully understand the products. Preying on investors' fears is common. In my opinion, a treasury security or CD can be a better choice, or at least an additional choice to consider, if someone is considering an equity index annuity.

So, to put things simply, there are three basic ways to hold money: cash, loan, or own. Let's have a look at each of them.

CASH

Many people, particularly young people, don't carry actual cash these days. They prefer to use their debit card for all purchases. However, when we speak of "cash" here, we're referring to the currency used to pay monthly expenses and dollars kept as emergency reserves in a checking, savings, or money market account. For peace of mind, we recommend people keep at least six months' worth of their income in an account that they can access without problems or penalties.

Sadly, most people in America today don't even have enough resources to pay their monthly bills, much less save six months of income. It's a huge problem. While I don't believe money buys happiness, being able to meet your obligations on a monthly basis can certainly provide tremendous peace of mind and is a starting point to build a future. Beyond that, having enough in an emergency fund for the day the air conditioner quits or your car suddenly breaks down is essential for your mental and emotional well-being.

For those short on cash, the first step, of course, is paring down your lifestyle, dealing with debt, and reorienting your priorities so you can meet your monthly obligations. Once you have enough money to pay your bills, start building up your cash reserves until you have six months of income. At this point, you are ready to invest for the future, and there are two primary ways you can do it: you can either *loan* your money as an investment, or you can *own* things as an investment.

LOAN

When you buy a CD (certificate of deposit) from a bank, the bank agrees to pay you a certain amount of interest over an agreed-upon timeframe. When the CD matures, you receive your money back. You've loaned your money to the bank to use as they choose until maturity.

You can also loan your money to a corporation by purchasing bonds in the corporation. Again, they promise to give you a certain rate of interest and your money back when the bond matures. In the same way, you can loan your money to the US government by purchasing bills, notes, or bonds.

You've perhaps heard that the US government owes a lot of money to China. This is because China has invested much of their excess capital in US government bonds. When those bonds mature, the US government will have to pay back the money plus interest. This is sometimes presented in the media as some kind of shady, back-room deal, but it isn't. Anyone can invest in US government bonds.

Some bonds have short maturities, while others mature after many years. The interest rate is determined by the creditworthiness of the issuer and what is called the "yield curve," which is what the specific bond pays for the maturity you decide to invest in.

US government bonds are considered guaranteed because they're backed by the full faith and credit—and, more importantly, the taxing power—of the US government. CDs and bank investments are covered by the FDIC, so they're guaranteed up to a certain limit. Corporate bonds aren't guaranteed, even though they are backed by the power of the corporation issuing them. Foreign government bonds are also an option, but credit quality and currency exchange rates are sometimes difficult to evaluate and require additional analysis.

If you're thinking about investing in a corporate bond, make sure you know the bond's rating. Ratings can be from Triple-A to what are called junk bonds. Junk bonds are most often associated with a startup or a speculative investment. They pay more interest, but the odds of getting your principal back is a lot lower than with a highly rated bond.

Municipal bond interest is federally tax-free and can be issued by a state, municipality, or county, which can be a good way to invest in your local community. If you happen to live in the same state in which the bond was issued, the interest is free from state income tax as well, which may make it a nice investment option, depending on your tax bracket and the stability of the issuer.

Since bonds are purchased with a pre-determined interest rate, you can estimate how much you will get back if you hold until maturity. When buying an individual bond with a fixed maturity date, you will know exactly what you're getting, as long as it's a high-quality bond that won't go bankrupt.

OWN

Besides loaning your money as an investment, you can also own things as an investment. Most people can relate to buying a home as an investment, but you can also own other things such as fine art and rare collectibles, as well as shares in a company. I learned about stocks as a child from my great aunt, who was born in 1901. As I shared in the introduction, she was friends with Russell Stover—

his candy store was located in our hometown of Kansas City—and she owned shares in his company.

Like bonds, there are many different types of stocks, and there are many different asset classes based on the capitalization and maturity of companies. Some stocks are considered "value companies," and others are considered "growth companies." Some of these companies exist in the US, and others exist internationally. Whatever the case, owning stock can give you an opportunity to participate in the ownership of the company.

WHICH INVESTMENT IS RIGHT?

The answer to that question is ultimately based upon your individual needs and investment goals. For some, short-term investing, which can mean loaning your money to banks by buying CDs or to the government by buying Treasury bills, could be considered the safest investment. However, others, who may be investing for the long term, may find that stock or ownership investments may allow them to build wealth in ways that cash reserves and providing loans can't provide.

Think of it this way: let's suppose you own a lawn-mowing business. Initially, you only own one lawn mower, but you do a great job, and your reputation grows. Suddenly, you find yourself with more yards than you can handle by yourself. Now, you have two choices. Either you refuse to accept any more customers, in which case your growth hits a plateau, or you hire more people, buy more lawn mowers, and grow your business.

What if you don't have the money to buy any extra lawn mowers or pay any extra workers? You still need access to capital so your business can grow. There are two things you can do.

First, you could go to family or friends and ask, "Can I borrow $1,000 to buy a few more lawn mowers and hire a few more people?" You create a business plan, showing exactly how you will generate income to pay them back, along with perhaps 10 percent interest.

Second, you could approach family or friends and offer to sell them half the company for $1,000. Now, you're not paying back a loan; instead, you're selling some of the equity in your company.

This is the essential difference between a bond (which is a loan) and a stock (which is ownership). When you buy bonds in a company, you are, in a sense, loaning the company money with the promise that they will pay you back, plus interest, at a specific date. If you buy stock in a company, you are buying an ownership interest in the company, which means you could participate in their upside as long as they continue to grow, for as long as you own your shares.

In the bond market, you can generally expect 3 to 5 percent returns per year on average, depending on the type of bonds. Since 1926, treasury bills have returned 3.4 percent and twenty-year government bonds have returned 5.5 percent.[6] On the other hand, the US stock market has averaged returns of 10 percent a year. That might not sound like a big difference. After all, the return on the bond market is relatively stable, while the stock market endures a lot more volatility. However, while the stock market doesn't grow in a straight line, it has consistently *trended* upward in the last hundred years and more. Difficult times have always proven to be short-term.

Here's an example I use to provide perspective: In 1950, when North Korea crossed the 38th parallel and invaded South Korea, the Dow was around 200. Today, in 2019, it stands at around 26,000. In the lifetime of someone who is now sixty-nine, that means the market is up 130 times. Not 130 percent, but 130 *times*. If anything, this shows that the market is a powerful wealth-building tool.

---

6 "2018 Fundamental for Investors," *Morningstar Managed Portfolios*, https://advisor.mp.morningstar.com/resourceDownload?type=publicForms&id=3f9df f3c-f085-47a1-98ba-0bc008df9f25.

OUR PROCESS

At Keen Wealth Advisors, once we've created a financial plan for a client, we next work to determine the proper ratio between stocks, bonds, and emergency reserves they need to make that plan work. These are decisions that should never be made from a hunch or a guess. They must be tailored to meet your specific financial plan.

There are over twenty different asset classes to consider, made up of various types of stocks, bonds, and alternative investments. While we feel certain the equity market is going to trend higher over time, we also know that there will be periods of difficulty. That's why we constantly advise clients against risky market-timing strategies or knee-jerk moves based on what's happening in the market or, worse yet, the headlines of the day. Our strategy of diversification, quantitative stock analysis, periodic adjustments, and short-term cash buckets for income needs is designed to help generate wealth for a family over decades, not days.

Time can play strange tricks on us when we're thinking about our investments. Remember sitting in class when you were a kid and the hour seemed to take an eternity but then summer would speed by? Our perception of time changes depending on what we are experiencing. Bull markets seem to fly by, while bear markets seem to last forever. However, market history tells us that the reverse is true.

Since the Great Depression, the average bull market lasted just over nine years, while the average bear market lasted 1.4 years. That includes the Great Depression-era data, which skews the average bear market data. Taking it one step further, the average bull market increase has been 473 percent while the average bear market's temporary decline has been roughly 41 percent.[7]

Remember, to date, time has been the healer. The markets have always returned to new highs after the temporary bear markets. Again, the Dow was around 200 in 1950. We have to be educated on the markets so that we can stay the course and weather the downturns so that you can be good stewards of your capital with an allocation that serves you.

Our goal is to create a portfolio and a process that will allow our clients not to be whipsawed by market cycles, that isn't chasing the asset that did best last year only to find it doing poorly the following year. We are patient, deliberate, and harness the cycles of various asset classes so a client can keep things in balance.

We believe it's best to keep things efficient, so we try to recommend that clients reduce unnecessary complex-

---

7 "History of U.S. Bear & Bull Markets Since 1926," *First Trust*, accessed March, 13, 2019, https://www.ftportfolios.com/Common/ContentFileLoader.aspx?ContentGUID=4ecfa978-d0bb-4924-92c8-628ff9bfe12d.

ity and costs in their long-term money. We generally use individual securities (stocks and bonds) along with what are called "indexes," which are designed to follow preset rules so the investment can track a specified basket of underlying holdings. By utilizing individual securities and indexes, we are able to help control the tax implications, as each client has their own unique cost basis in each security, which allows us to be proactive on the timing of taking gains and losses. In our opinion, it's smarter to have a globally diversified portfolio than to invest solely in the US market, and in most cases, we discourage our clients from using mutual funds.

THE PROBLEM WITH MUTUAL FUNDS

We don't like using mutual funds for several reasons. The first has to do with cost. When you sit down with a financial advisor to discuss investing in a mutual fund, always ask them for the *total cost* of the plan they're putting together, including their own advisor fees. Often, either they will tell you a half-truth, or they simply don't know. That's because a good many mutual funds tend to be significantly more expensive than people realize.

If you own a mutual fund, you will pay fees inside the fund, as well as transaction costs. Some of these fees are easy to find in the prospectus, but some are buried deep in the small print. Your total cost in fees for a mutual fund can easily be over 1 or 2 percent or more of your *total investment* annually.[8] Your financial advisor may also charge between 1 and 1.5 percent to manage your mutual funds.

Suddenly, you find that you've engaged in something that is consuming upwards of 3 to 4 percent of your total investment in fees alone each year. If you ask the advisor up front for the total cost, they will probably only tell you about their specific advisor fees. This kind of half-truth is fairly common in the industry.

A second reason we don't like to use mutual funds is because promoted historical returns may be misleading regarding potential future performance. When a fund has a good year, it tends to attract a lot of money, because people generally look at recent performance when deciding where to invest. Once the fund attracts a ton of money, it becomes bloated, and now it simply may be impossible to replicate its previous performance. You've now invested in a substandard fund.

We've also seen fund companies seeding many funds over time, then closing the funds that do poorly and keeping and promoting the ones that happen to do good. This practice can cause an investor to believe that the fund will replicate its performance, when it may have just been

8 Kenneth Kim, "How Much Do Mutual Funds Really Cost?" *Forbes*, September 24, 2016, https://www.forbes.com/sites/kennethkim/2016/09/24/how-much-do-mutual-funds-really-cost.

luck or random. We see people chasing performance in mutual funds all the time, and their returns are almost always disappointing.

A third factor that can be detrimental to a mutual fund investor is inefficient tax ramifications. Consider the complexity of tracking gains and losses inside of a pooled product where tens of thousands of participants own units of the pool. Each year the fund is required to add up all of the gains and losses for each security that the fund had for the current tax year and pass those tax consequences to the unit holders proportionately. The fund may have long-term gains on holdings that it decides to sell in a given year, and the taxes on those gains will be paid by the current unit holders—even if the unit holders didn't receive the gain! These are called *inherited tax liabilities*, and they should be avoided at all cost.

Imagine buying into a fund this year and potentially being down on your investment, but still receiving a tax bill for gains—gains you didn't receive. We've seen this especially in volatile years like 2002 and 2009. Many unsuspecting investors in taxable accounts learn about this the hard way.

TREAD CAREFULLY

How many stories have we read about lottery winners

who go bankrupt within a few short, tragic years? The same thing happens to superstar athletes—they sign huge contracts and then lose it all quickly.

You have to be ready for the responsibility that comes with generating wealth. In my home, I'm a big believer in being respectful of resources. I annoy my loved ones by constantly making them turn off lights when they leave rooms, by encouraging them not to waste food or take two drinks out of a water bottle and then trash it, and not to leave outside doors open when it's hot or cold. This may be a product of my childhood. Though these might seem like trivial things, I believe it's important to learn to be responsible even with small things. If you can't handle having a little bit of money, you won't be able to handle having a lot.

The investment world is like a vortex. If you make uninformed decisions with no strategy or direction, an endless number of plain bad investments or even scams are waiting to wash all your money away like the storm surge in a hurricane. If you want to generate wealth and maintain it, you have to be ready to take responsibility for every financial decision you make. Even I have had to learn this lesson the hard way.

Financial advising has been my core business for twenty-seven years, but early on I was presented with a couple of opportunities to become a silent partner on outside business opportunities. As a silent partner, I didn't have to take any time away from my primary business. I simply had to invest capital and report it once a quarter.

One of those opportunities was a real estate development company, and the second was a one-hundred-year-old manufacturing company in Kansas City. Though I had no expertise in either industry, I put my capital on the line, and I even signed personal guarantees on those investments, which is a legal promise to repay debt.

Unfortunately, I made the real estate investment shortly before the real estate market crashed. Suddenly, I found myself pouring more money into the real estate development company on a monthly basis. As for the manufacturing company, I bought in on the encouragement of a trusted advisor, but I later learned that the advisor had been keeping information from me. Within a year, I learned the company was close to failing.

Both of these investments cost me more money than I care to say, and produced a substantial amount of stress and anxiety. Fortunately, I was able to exit both of them, but I learned an important lesson. Outside of your core business or industry, you are essentially in kindergarten. When you make investment decisions in an area that you don't fully understand, you are opening yourself up to devastating consequences. Tread carefully into new waters!

SO, YOU WANT TO GO IT ALONE?

Some people prefer to go it alone, making their own investment decisions without the input of or investment in a financial advisor. You can certainly do this, and there are any number of tools you can use to educate yourself online. Bear in mind, making smart financial decisions is about more than simply educating yourself on the options. You also have to develop the emotional fortitude to stick with your plan. Since you won't have a financial advisor constantly encouraging you to stay on track, you will have to be self-motivated. Personally, I prefer to have someone holding me accountable, but you might have the strength of will to do this yourself. If so, more power to you.

Managing money on an island, alone, is toughest when the market is going through difficult times, because the media will bombard you with apocalyptic warnings. There is an endless amount of information at our fingertips these days, along with resources and tools. It can be time-consuming to wade through them all, but it's certainly possible, if you're willing and able. Still, you have to learn how to manage your emotions in these hectic times.

As I said, I've always preferred to have someone in my

corner, providing constant encouragement and focus. You see, it's about more than simply making investment decisions. There's a psychology behind managing money effectively, as we will address in more detail next.

Chapter Nine

MANAGE MARKET PSYCHOLOGY

I believe success begins with developing a long-term perspective. Many of the clients I've worked with started with nothing, but they've saved and lived within their means over the years. They've watched their wealth ebb and flow with the market cycles. They've been through it all, and because of that, they have developed long-term perspectives that have helped them realize their own individual successes.

What year were you born? Go back and look at what the Dow Jones Industrial Average was in January of the year you were born. This can be found with a simple Google search. See how far it's come. I like to use this exercise with clients because it gives them a clear understanding of how the market has created wealth over the long haul, despite short-term fluctuations.

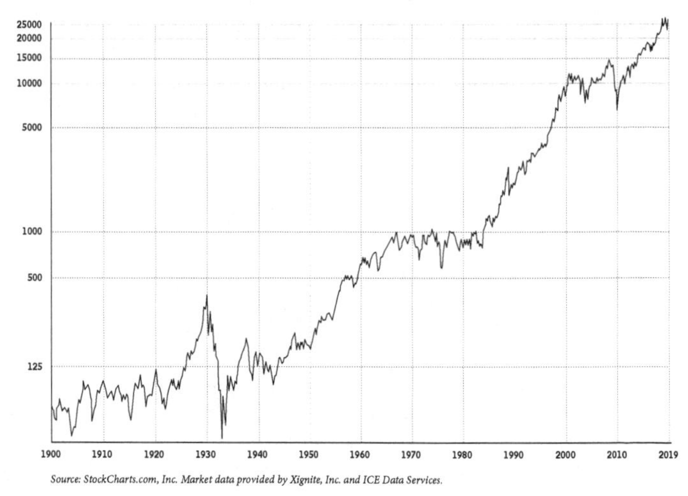

If you break it down since 1926, you will find that small cap stocks have made more than large cap stocks, and *substantially* more than long-term bonds, treasury bills, inflation, and gold. Over the last hundred years, you would have averaged 10 percent growth per year in the equity market.[9] Imagine if you were Rip Van Winkle. You could invest your money, sleep for thirty years, and wake up with a great deal more money.

However, we live in an emotional world, and every single minute of the day, we are bombarded with information about the markets, money, and the future, which creates a lot of anxiety, especially for people approaching retire-

9 "2018 Fundamental for Investors," *Morningstar Managed Portfolios*, https://advisor.mp.morningstar.com/resourceDownload?type=publicForms&id=3f9dff3c-f085-47a1-98ba-0bc008df9f25.

ment. As retirement approaches and the reality hits you that you're going to have to live off your investments for the rest of your life, it's easy to worry that a market downturn will destroy your wealth overnight. If you've made bad investments when you were younger, it only makes the anxiety more intense.

If we learn from the mistakes of our past, then they aren't failures—they are the pathway to answers. If you've had investments for a few decades, how did you respond in 1987 when the market had a "Black Monday?" How did you respond in 2001 and 2002 after 9/11, Enron's failure, and WorldCom's demise? Did you panic and sell at the bottom? What about 2008 and 2009 during the financial crises as Lehman failed and Bernie Madoff was exposed?

We learn the most from expensive mistakes because they demand our attention. However, as you approach retirement, you have to stop making expensive mistakes. You no longer have enough time to learn and recover. Maybe your investments have weathered the last thirty or forty years, but an emotional mistake could still blow them off course, and you don't have forty years to make them back.

THE BIG MISTAKES

The biggest mistake people can make is selling investments at the wrong time. If you've set up a plan and know that you have enough capital outside of the stock market to cover your income needs for a specific number of years, then you should find that it's okay to hold onto your stock investments when the market goes through a correction. You may also find that you're actually in a position to invest more, or certainly to rebalance, because as history has taught us, the market will eventually rebound.

Another big mistake people make is to move all of their money into one specific sector because it happens to be the hot place to be. They're feeling euphoric, and they think, "Wow, I have to make the most of this opportunity right now, or I'll miss out." Then the bubble bursts.

In the late 1990s, a group of people working for a local technology company were advised by a coworker in their company, who wasn't a licensed financial advisor, to move all of their money into a particular tech fund. The fund had grown by 50 percent the previous year, so it seemed like a good idea. Sadly, when the tech bubble burst, the fund melted down, and by the time these people came to us for help, they had lost two-thirds of their retirement savings, all because they tried to chase the tech bubble—seeking short-term success instead of long-term consistency.

BEWARE OF YOUR BIASES

There are biases that can negatively influence your decision-making in ways you might not be aware of. For example, *recency bias* refers to a tendency to think that recent events or trends will continue in the future. We saw this coming out of the economic woes of 2008 and 2009, when many people assumed that the market's downturn would continue indefinitely, and made investment decisions accordingly. Recency bias can cause us to make rash decisions.

Confirmation bias occurs when we seek out information to confirm what we already believe. For example, someone might choose a news station based on their political beliefs—they want to hear the news filtered in a way that confirms their existing views. We do this far more often than we admit to ourselves, garnering opinions and looking for research that agrees with us.

By the way, studies have shown that making investment decisions based on politics leads to poor performance.[10] We often see people make knee-jerk decisions based on election results, but after a twenty-seven-year career, I have never seen any correlation between who gets elected—Democrat or Republican—and how the equity markets or bond markets perform. While there might be

10 Bespoke Investment Group, "Politics And Investing: Keep Them Separate," *Seeking Alpha*, October 31, 2017, https://seekingalpha.com/article/4118373-politics-investing-keep-separate.

a short-term adjustment, I have never seen any long-term or lasting change.

We once had someone introduced to us as a potential client who was so upset when a certain president got elected that he sold *all* of his equity investments out of his diversified portfolio. We did everything we could to help him understand that he wasn't hurting the newly elected president—he was compromising his family's future. He had started with over $2 million in his portfolio that would have carried him for the rest of his life, but he sold out close to the bottom of the market. In the years afterward, the markets went on to make new highs. There was nothing we could do for him after the fact, and we didn't end up taking him on as a client. I believe he ended up keeping all of his money in CDs, paying 1 percent. At the rate he needed to spend, he would not have come close to meeting his family's needs.

AVOID EMOTIONAL MISTAKES

The best way to avoid all of these emotional mistakes is to create a financial plan that lays out what you're trying to accomplish and why. This takes your focus off the day-to-day market fluctuations and headlines and keeps you moving toward your long-term goals. Based on that financial plan, you then create a *balanced* portfolio using predetermined parameters, which eliminates emotion from your decision-making.

Don't mistake a decline in the market for a permanent downturn. Past performance certainly doesn't guarantee future results, but as of 2019, every single decline in the market to date has been temporary. More importantly, every decline in the last two hundred years has presented opportunity, but you won't get the chance to take advantage of these opportunities unless you've put parameters in place to prevent emotional reactions.

During the financial crisis of 2008 and 2009, it is estimated that Warren Buffett was personally down in value approximately *$23 billion*. My question to you is: *how much money did Warren Buffett permanently lose during that time?* We have the benefit of hindsight when answering this question as we know that the answer is none—because he didn't sell.[11]

Remain steady during market corrections! Stick to your plan, and stay within your parameters. By setting up your financial plan in advance, you're more prepared for whatever comes at you next week, or next month, in the marketplace. Commit to your plans with confidence, and be intentional with all of the decisions that you make along the way.

11 Stephanie Loiacono, "Rules That Warren Buffett Lives By," *Investopedia*, May 2, 2018, https://www.investopedia.com/financial-edge/0210/rules-that-warren-buffett-lives-by.aspx.

Chapter Ten

PREPARE FOR MARKET CORRECTIONS

A crusty old gentleman walked into my office in the middle of 2000, looking for an advisor. He had some very specific questions, and he had already met with several other financial advisors. He was a well-respected executive at his firm, whose job was in compliance. Some of his coworkers dreaded seeing him coming, but they respected his straightforward attitude.

I worked with him over a period of time, and we got to know one another fairly well. He retired shortly before 9/11. It was a tragic time, and we can all remember where we were when those awful events happened. This particular gentleman had spent forty years at work, planned carefully for his retirement, diversified his portfolio with a combination of stock and bonds, and then watched the equity side of his portfolio tank in the months immediately afterward in 2001.

Ultimately, the market came back up, but then, in the midst of his retirement, he saw the markets tank again in 2008 and 2009. He has now been retired nineteen years, and he has lived through two of the worst market corrections in history.

Fortunately, he understood that the strategies he'd put in place were enough to supplement his Social Security and provide for his monthly needs, so he didn't panic. He didn't sell his equity investments. Instead, he knew that the equity markets will occasionally experience downturns, but historically, they've always been temporary. Consequently, he knew that if he didn't sell those parts of his portfolio, he would come out stronger. He also had the experience of forty years of saving and investing, which had given him a long-term perspective that helped him navigate during the down times.

THE TREND OF EQUITY MARKETS

Just because someone has been saving and investing for forty years doesn't mean they are immune to panic. It's one thing to save money while you're working, but when you approach retirement, suddenly the possibility of a downward market becomes a more terrifying prospect.

After all, you've never been retired before. You don't have any experience responding to market volatility as a retired person until it happens to you. We can alleviate much of this fear by helping you develop a historical perspective on the markets, helping you to see past the dips and peaks to the overall trends.

One of the questions we often get from clients is, "Can anyone know when a market correction is coming?" If you have an asset class that has grown an average of 10 percent a year over a long period of time, it might swing as much as 40 to 50 percent from time to time. Wouldn't it be nice to anticipate when the market is going to peak, so you could get out, then wait for it to bottom out, so you could get back in?

Unfortunately, no one has been able to do this consistently. No computer algorithm, no expert, not even Warren Buffet, has been able to predict those entry and exit points consistently. However, we do know from history that the market has always trended upward, with the volatility acting like a rubber band fixed around the trendline.[12]

There are plenty of people who will tell you they've figured it out, that they have a secret way, some mathematical formula or system for determining exactly when

12 Siegel, Jeremy, *Stock for the Long Run*, (New York: McGraw-Hill, 1994)

the market will shift in one direction or the other, but they are all snake-oil salesmen. Even Warren Buffett failed to predict the bottom of the market in 2008. He made investments around the halfway point, then watched the markets continue to sink.

In the lifetime of a sixty-nine-year-old born in 1950, the Dow Jones has grown from 200 to 26,000, as of March 2019.[13] If anything, that shows what a powerful machine the market has been. Has this all happened by chance, or is there something at work here, some force producing this consistent growth that indicates it will continue?

As it turns out, there is something else that has grown by almost the same percentage over the same period of time: corporate earnings. The earnings of the companies that make up the markets are the biggest contributing factor in the growth of the markets.[14] The work that we are all doing in our various specializations, as we do business nationally and globally, is helping to create a higher standard of living for most people and is also helping by contributing to the overall growth of the markets.

If you want to follow something important and not be

---

13 "Dow Jones - 100 Year Historical Chart," *Macrotrends*, https://www.macrotrends.net/1319/dow-jones-100-year-historical-chart, accessed April 8, 2019.

14 "Corporate Profits After Tax (without IVA and CCAdj)," *FRED*, March 28, 2019, https://fred.stlouisfed.org/series/CP.

distracted by the media and headlines of the day, consider watching the earnings over time of the companies that make up your portfolio.

DEALING WITH MARKET CORRECTIONS

From 1980 to 2018, there's been a 14 percent correction in the market each year.[15] That means, in each year, there's usually a point where the market dips 14 percent lower than its previous high before heading back up again. Over the very long term, there also tends to be a major correction about every thirty years, although, as mentioned earlier, there have been two such of these downturns in the past fifteen years. Since we know this, we know that investors might have to wait it out a little longer than usual. When a major correction hits, it might take multiple years for the market to recover, but, as history has shown, it does recover.

Market corrections are typically always uncomfortable. Waiting them out feels a bit like being a kid in class watching the clock and waiting for the school day to end—every second feels like an eternity.

These are the emotions we grapple with when the market fluctuates. When it's to the upside, we operate on auto-

15 "Guide to the Markets," *J.P. Morgan*, December 31, 2018, https://am.jpmorgan.com/gi/getdoc/1383598874518.

pilot. When it starts dipping downward, suddenly we're biting our fingernails, anxious every day, wondering, "How low will it go? Will it ever come back up?" With the internet, we can find ourselves checking the market *constantly* during a downward correction. This isn't good for your mental or emotional health. Although we want people to be proactive and responsible, it's never good to spend every minute of the day checking the market.

When I first entered this business in the early 1990s, clients only received a quarterly statement in the mail. If they wanted to see their balance more often, they had to call and request the information, which most people just simply didn't do.

Today, all of the information is at our fingertips at all times, and it's not always a good thing. This is where recency bias comes into play. Some people will start doing calculations, assuming that the most recent trend will continue indefinitely: "If the market keeps dropping at this rate, we will be at zero in another thirty months!" As an aside, it's also not good to do this when the market is spiking higher, saying to yourself, "If the market keeps this up, we will be way ahead of plan, so let's increase our spending now."

When you find yourself in this state of mind, it's important to stick with your plan. Don't panic, don't sell when the market is down, and don't fall prey to the upside hype.

MAINTAIN A FIXED INCOME

If you have no strategy, and no pre-committed actions, then it's easier to make rash decisions. That's why it's so important to set the parameters before you ever encounter any problems. You won't have to worry about repositioning things because you'll already know what you're doing. Preset parameters help you avoid getting into a death spiral of emotional investment decisions.

Beyond that, you have to prepare yourself for market corrections. We believe it is important to have a minimum of five years of your income needs in fixed income or bonds—investments that are considered to be stable and shouldn't go down violently during difficult times in the stock market. This bucket of funds should be enough to carry you through the uneasy market corrections. A fixed amount you can depend on also insulates you from needing to sell investments at a bad time in order to have money to live on.

Five years is the *minimum*. Some of our clients have ten, fifteen, even twenty years of income in fixed income, which makes it easier to view their equity investments as long-term money that they don't need to touch. We prefer basing this fixed income amount on what you need to live on rather than using some impersonal percentage. There's a psychological power that comes from knowing your monthly needs will be met. If your needs are met, you're also in a better position to rebalance and buy when the market is down, which may allow you to take advantage of the growth when the market recovers.

If we've learned anything from market bubbles, it's that you need a balanced portfolio. Never bet on one security. When there's volatility in the market, if you're following your plan, you may find that you could actually harness that volatility. Buy some when the market is low, and when there's growth, move some of the profit into the more stable parts of your portfolio.

LIFEBOAT DRILLS

At our firm, we like to do what we call "lifeboat drills," where we try to prepare for the next inevitable downturn. Although you can never know for sure when a downturn will happen or what it will look like, you know it's coming sooner or later. Fortunately, you don't need to know the *when* and *where*. Setting yourself up to prosper through any market environment is possible, as long as you have a plan and you're disciplined.

Your portfolio might not be there yet. You might need some financial help to rebalance your investments. It's a lot easier to stick with your plan when you have faith in it, which is why we strongly believe in using a financial advisor. We've seen too many people try to do this on their own, and they often end up panicking and bailing on their strategy at the wrong time, because they don't trust themselves. When they see that 20 or 30 percent of their equity portfolio has vanished, they think, "I messed up. I made the wrong investment decisions, and now I'm ruined!"

If you decide to work with an advisor, find someone who can help you make high-level, tactical decisions about your investment goals based on the context of your personal financial blueprint. Doing this can allow you to gain a clear sense of *why* your personalized investment model is allocating funds to various asset classes. At our firm, we prefer to process information in-house so we can provide answers for every investment decision. If you understand what's happening on your behalf with your investments, you should be able to feel a lot more confident during the tough times.

Even though no one can predict the next market correction perfectly, a financial advisor should be able to separate the news from the noise to understand what is happening in the markets. That's why my wife and I work with advisors ourselves. Even though I've created many of the processes in our firm, I still like to have my advisors walk with us through our own financial planning.

Even with twenty-seven years of experience, I still benefit from having the objective views, counsel, and guidance of my financial advisory team. I strongly recommend you do the same, but you shouldn't work with just anyone. You need to find the financial advisor who is right for you.

Chapter Eleven

PICK A FINANCIAL ADVISOR

At the old bank-owned brokerage firms I used to work for, instead of speaking about clients as people, companies often talked about "increasing wallet share" and making "same-store sales." At my firm, each of our clients becomes a member of our family. We get to know them. We care about them and want them to do well in life. I don't allow people to talk about increasing wallet share. That is offensive to me. We aren't a sales organization; we're a consulting and people organization.

Be very selective about the advisory firm you choose to work with. Make sure that the custodian who handles your assets isn't owned by the same company that is directing the investments and accounts. This sets up a potential Bernie Madoff scenario. Remember, Madoff had custody of his clients' assets. There were no third-party checks and balances, which enabled him to print statements and steal money. Nobody knew any better until the 2008 market collapse exposed him.

Make sure the custodian of your assets is independent, and never write a check for an investment directly to your advisor. Other than possibly paying for hourly planning fees, a check should always be made out to a third-party custodian, such as Charles Schwab, Fidelity, TD Ameritrade, or Pershing.

FIDUCIARY VS. SUITABILITY STANDARD

When selecting an advisor, find out if they are a fiduciary or if they are acting under the suitability standard. A fiduciary has a legal obligation to do what is in your best interest all the time, in every situation. On the other hand, the suitability standard merely states that an investment must be "suitable" at the time of sale. The bar is low—a broker can ask a client six or seven questions over the course of a ten-minute meeting and decide that an investment is legally suitable—even though it might have higher fees and provide under-the-table kickbacks to the salesperson.

An advisor operating under the suitability standard has a lot of leeway for recommending investments that aren't in the client's best interest. Some advisors can even wear both hats. They will operate as a fiduciary one minute, and then the next minute they will act as a salesperson for a specific investment. If you don't know what to ask, you can never be sure when they are switching hats.

This is a questionable practice we see all too often in this industry. An advisor working for Company A will recommend an investment product from Company B to a client, and because there are two different companies involved, the client won't see any conflict of interest. However, buried somewhere in the fine print is the revelation that Company B is owned by Company A—information that is not otherwise disclosed to the client. In that case, the advisor is getting an advisory fee from the client, as well as fees, commissions, or kickbacks for recommending company investment products. It's a massive conflict of interest that isn't readily apparent.

Under the suitability standard, there's a lot of "pay to play" shenanigans. Sometimes, a firm won't offer a company's investment product on their platform unless the company pays a lot of money, and then, because the company is paying a lot of money, advisors at the firm are encouraged to push that specific product. Remember, the product only has to be legally suitable *at the time of sale*. The onus is on the client to determine when the product is no longer suitable.

In contrast, a fiduciary advisor has a legal obligation to make sure everything they recommend is in the client's best interest, and the onus is on the advisor to make sure things continue to be in the client's best interest as the relationship evolves.

Some people are jaded about the financial industry, which I completely understand, but others are far too trusting. They assume that any financial advisor they deal with has their best interests in mind. While there are some very good brokers, in many of the cases, they are still salespeople pushing products with no real financial planning being offered, so clients aren't getting the type of service they may believe they're getting.

WHAT TO ASK YOUR FINANCIAL ADVISOR

Liking your advisor isn't enough. Of course, having rapport and a friendly relationship with an advisor is important, but there are some questions I strongly encourage you to ask them.

Here are my recommendations:

- What kind of education do you provide clients?

At Keen Wealth, we offer an educational podcast called *Keen On Retirement*, which is available on iTunes and our website KeenOnRetirement.com. We also put out a new blog post every other week that is purely educational in nature. Throughout the year, we offer classes on Social Security, taxes, Medicare coverage, financial planning for retirement, spending, and much more. We offer these courses to help people understand the basic concepts of planning and investing. I believe *every* responsible financial advisor should do the same. It's a vital part of serving clients, so be sure to ask.

- What kind of continuing education do you do yourself?

A financial advisor should be required to attend regular coursework, and not just the minimum. The Managing Director and Chief Investment Officer at our firm, Matt Wilson, who has worked with me since 2002, joins me at the invitation-only Barron's Top Advisors Summit each year. We learn from some of the brightest professionals in the industry, share best practices with other top advisors, and compare notes. Our advisor team also attends other professional development sessions and think-tank groups, because we're committed to being ongoing learners. Each of our firm's advisors either has the CFP® designation or is on a track to achieve that designation. These credentials require consistent, ongoing continuing education as well.

- What kinds of questions do you ask clients?

You can tell a lot about a financial advisor during your first meeting by the questions they ask you. Do they only want your financial statements? Do they want to see your assets right off the bat? Do they only talk numbers, or do they ask more personal questions? Do they ask you about your goals for the future? Do they ask about your upbringing, your family dynamic, your family's financial situation when you were growing up? Do they ask about the dynamics between family members?

All of these personal questions are important, because they can come into play as you start planning and preparing for your future. With this kind of information, a good advisor can identify patterns in your personal history that help them see around corners. They should ask questions about your legacy goals, about your healthcare, insurance, tax history, about your relationship with your spouse, parents, and children. Statements, investments, and assets, while important, are secondary to a client's personal life, experience, and goals. If an advisor goes straight to the numbers during a first meeting, it's typically a red flag. They may be using perceived financial planning as a sales tool for investment products.

If you're meeting with an advisor and they keep looking at their watch, that's also generally a red flag. At Keen Wealth, we don't allow our advisors to have their phones when meeting with a client. We don't want them checking the time, or checking messages, or getting distracted in any other way. Just because an advisor turns his phone upside down on the desk doesn't mean it's not still a distraction. A financial advisor should be fully attentive and invested in getting to know and understand a client, not distracted or rushed.

- What is the total cost to a client?

Many advisors fail to reveal the total cost to their clients and may grossly misrepresent the total cost to prospective clients. Worse, a good portion of these advisors don't know the total cost themselves.

You shouldn't ask an advisor, "What are your fees?" Instead, ask something like, "What will my total costs be to work with you?" Remember, the advisor's fees are just a portion of your total cost. You will also pay fees and expenses for the underlying investments they recommend. Some of these fees and expenses show up on your monthly or quarterly statements, but in many cases, they are not in plain sight. It's important to have a full understanding of how all of these costs add up, as they are a very real headwind to your net returns. It's also important to compare apples to apples when interviewing and evaluating advisors.

There can be many different fees and expenses levied

on your accounts. Many brokers are still charging commissions per trade for securities or even front-load or back-end loads on mutual funds and annuities. These loads can be as high as 10 percent on these types of products.

You may have heard the term "no-load" mutual fund, which simply means there is no commission to invest or withdraw funds. That does not mean that there are no fees. Even no-load funds have ongoing management fees and internal transaction charges. The management fees can be found in the prospectus, but the transaction charges must be found in the fund's statement of additional information. These can be hard to find, and harder to decipher, but the costs are very real. Most investors and many advisors don't know where to look for these charges.

There are other investment products such as non-traded REITs, hedge funds, and private equity that have large commissions and ongoing fees that can seriously eat into an investor's returns. Most investors should tread very lightly when considering these types of investments.

At the end of the day, make sure to get an honest and accurate answer regarding the total cost of doing business with each advisor.

- Do you use a checklist-driven process to advise families?

Surgeons use checklists. Pilots use checklists. Engineers use checklists. If a financial advisor isn't using a checklist, it's a problem. You don't need to see the checklist in detail, but you should make sure it exists. No advisor can remember everything, no matter how sharp they are. There are simply too many details that need to be looked at for a family in any given period of time.

Keen Wealth Advisors

Perceptive. Personalized. Precise.

Client Review Agenda

Personal Update

- What is your outlook for the future?
- What gives you concern today?
- Any changes in your life since our last review?
- Any changes in family status (i.e., births, marriage, death, or divorce)
- Any changes in your general health?
- Any changes in your job or career?
- Any anticipated changes in your life expected in the future?

Financial Update

- Review Financial Plan
  - Review goals, objectives, and changes to financial situation
  - Review and update personal financial statement
  - Confirm understanding of cash flow needs
- Discuss Investment Portfolios
  - Current asset allocations
  - Performance
  - Investment objectives
- Tax Planning
  - Qualified Plans (401k, 403b, Roth IRA, etc.)
  - Tax-loss harvesting
  - Withholding

Risk Management

- Review current life insurance policies/coverage
- Discussion of long-term care insurance
- Review short & long-term disability
- Property/casualty & liability

Estate Planning

- Beneficiary designation review
- Wills/Trusts/Power of Attorney/HIPAA/Health Care Surrogate
- Stretch IRA provisions
- Charities or civic groups you are interested in (Donor Advised Fund)
- Family foundations

6201 College Blvd • Suite 325 • Overland Park, KS 66211
Main 913-624-1841 • www.KeenWealthAdvisors.com

COMMITMENT TO YOUR WELL-BEING

Being a financial advisor is a great privilege. We get close to the families we work with, watch them grow and change. Most of the things we deal with are positive—clients enjoying their lives, experiencing the freedom their careful, consistent investing has afforded them. We also walk with clients through some difficult times. Real life happens, and we get to help people plan, prepare, and endure the hardships.

You need a financial advisor who is committed to your well-being, who sees value in a relationship and will stick with you through all of life's changes.

PART THREE

ENJOY THE BEST HALF OF YOUR LIFE

Chapter Twelve

STAY ACTIVE

Recently, I received a call in my office, and when I looked at the caller ID, I saw the name of a client's husband. Although we have a great relationship with both spouses, this raised an alarm because typically the wife was the one to call in. I had known these clients for over twelve years, and the husband had never called me. Before I picked up the phone, I knew something was wrong.

As it turned out, the wife had been diagnosed with a rare form of cancer out of the blue and given three to six months to live. While this was tragic news, it wasn't completely unexpected. If there's anything I've learned over the course of my career, it's that all people deal with hardships in life.

We never know how our individual journeys will play out. A few days after receiving this news, I found myself sitting at the kitchen table in the client's home with one of my financial planners. We wanted to make sure that all aspects of the client's financial plan were in order.

This particular husband and wife had retired when they were in their early fifties, and when someone retires that early, it's always a point of concern because of the longer time period to make their assets last. A lot more work must be done up front to ensure they will have the resources they need to last for the rest of their lives.

The husband had a nice government pension, while the wife had worked as an engineer and built a retirement portfolio. They owned a farm and had the resources to retire early and pursue their passions. As deeply involved members of their church, they planned to go on mission trips and travel the world.

Eleven years after retirement, the wife received her diagnosis, and I met with them to make sure their financial plans were accurate and up to date. I've been through similar situations many times with clients, and they always look me in the eye and ask the same question, "Will my spouse be taken care of when I'm gone?"

They're worried that someone will take advantage of the surviving spouse, that scammers will come out of the woodwork and find ways to get their hands on the money. In those instances, they turn to their trusted advisors, looking for someone to protect their assets as best they can so the surviving spouse will be financially secure for the rest of their life.

By the end of that two-hour meeting, we were all feeling the weight of the decisions that had to be made. We hugged. There were tears. It was real life, and I felt honored to be entrusted with this family's future. We had developed a relationship of sincerity and trust over many years, so the wife knew we would do the right thing for her loved ones. At the same time, they were both incredibly grateful that they'd been able to enjoy eleven wonderful years of retirement. They saw the positive more than the negative.

LEAVE EVERYTHING ON THE FIELD

As a result of these experiences, I often tell clients, "Stay active and engaged as long as possible during the next phase of your life. Enjoy each day to the fullest, leaving everything on the field as they say. Don't look forward to some magic day in the future when you will have enough money to enjoy life. Plan for the future, yes, but enjoy life *now*. Enjoy every day."

Not everyone can retire at fifty, of course—or at sixty, for that matter—so try to enjoy the journey along the way.

When you create a plan for the future that is measurable, it allows you to enjoy every day, because you know you're working toward something with intention and vision.

I recently turned fifty myself, and I can safely say that it's an interesting age. You start to realize that even if you live to a normal life expectancy, there are only about thirty Christmases and New Year's Days left. Even if the futurists are right, and we all wind up living to 120, we all still have an end date. Time is limited, and, more than that, it's a precious commodity.

At age forty-nine and a half, I received my AARP membership card in the mail at the office, and it startled me. "Wow, I guess I'm a member of the AARP now," I thought. I later learned that one of my team members had signed me up six months early as a joke. Still, I keep that card in my desk as a reminder to live each day to the fullest, to stay active and take care of my health, even as I plan for the future.

Fortunately, I see many people thriving in retirement. They are active and involved with their passions, feeding their souls and enjoying life fully. One of my clients retired in 2003, and he's still going strong. He has been in retirement for nearly sixteen years, as of the writing of this book, and he's no homebody. He routinely drives race cars with a professional driver at a track near his home. He also volunteers for the Boys Scouts of America, and he's an avid golfer. He is enjoying an active life and loving it.

Despite this, he did face a moment of decision early in his retirement when his wife passed away. It was unexpected, and he had to make some difficult decisions going forward. In his grief, he could easily have become a recluse. Often, when a spouse dies, social networks change, and the surviving spouse loses contact with many people. It happened to this gentleman, and he found himself leaning heavily into his faith community as he developed new friends who were also widows and widowers.

He eventually came out of his grieving process and continued to live life to the fullest. He exercises at his local community center every day, and he's still going strong at eighty years old.

ADJUSTING TO THE POST-WORK LIFE

Many of our engineering clients are dedicated to their work. Unlike people in many other industries, engineers typically don't view their jobs as drudgery or a "necessary evil." They love what they do, so it's hard for some of them to retire. They are leaving behind something they enjoy, and, more than that, their identity is wrapped up in their profession. In many cases, they've done some truly impressive work that has made a difference in the world.

Many of our clients regularly get up at five in the morning and put in a twelve-hour work day without complaining. They are intense, focused, and committed. As we like to tell them, once they retire, they can take all of the time they used to fill with work and focus on their health, family, passions, and spiritual well-being.

Those who thrive in retirement typically have a protocol in the morning for getting up and being active. It might be as simple as a routine walk around the neighborhood, but even a mile or two of walking can make a huge difference. My clients who are thriving get involved in places like their local community center or the YMCA, where they take swimming or cycling classes. Medicare will often cover those expenses because they are health-related.

THE IMPORTANCE OF HAVING AN AGENDA

It's best to enter retirement with some plan for what your days will look like. You now have freedom and flexibility, yet there's a solace that comes from routine. Though it might seem like a contradiction, we need both stability and variety for a balanced life.

In my experience, retirees who have a routine wakeup

time, workout time, and a plan for major activities each week tend to be happier and more fulfilled. They also thrive by engaging in social interaction. Without the accustomed daily work routine, it's too easy to become a recluse during retirement. Many of our engineer clients are introverts by nature, so unless they have a plan for getting out there and interacting with people, they tend to withdraw. This isn't a good dynamic for mental or emotional well-being. Therefore, it's vital to lean into your social network, which may include a hobby or sport, a charitable organization or faith community.

HEALTHY LIFESTYLE

Attending to one's health is also a priority. Many people entering retirement aren't used to visiting the doctor for checkups. However, it has become more common for people to begin yearly checkups as they enter their fifties. This should continue, even more so, during retirement. Embracing a healthy lifestyle includes regular appointments with your primary care physician, your dermatologist, and other specialists who can catch problems early.

Following a healthy diet will serve you well. Good food enhances life, and in retirement there's more time to seek out and prepare healthy meals. There's also more time for social dining and trying new foods, especially when traveling. These days, more people are becoming aware of heart-healthy food choices, and more restaurants are offering healthy selections on their menus. We eat for both pleasure and nutrition, so find the foods that satisfy both your taste buds and your health needs, and enjoy!

THE KEY TO A HAPPY RETIREMENT

A study in the journal *Nature Human Behaviour* determined that you need between $60,000 and $75,000 annual income to be happy.[16] This is the sweet spot for positive daily emotions. It means your bills are paid, you're not stressed out about meeting your needs, and there's enough left over to enjoy life a little bit. This was the first study I have seen that places a number on the extent that money can buy happiness. Beyond that, the study argues, more money won't buy more happiness.

SOCIAL NETWORKING

Once you have enough money to comfortably meet all of your needs, your happiness and well-being are most influenced by your social support system. At our firm, we believe so strongly in this that we created the Keen Wealth Community, providing educational and social events for our clients. It began with our annual holiday

16 Ducharme, Jamie. "This Is the Amount of Money You Need to Be Happy, According to Research." *Money*, February 14, 2018, http://time.com/money/5157625/ideal-income-study/.

event in December, which is a festive client get-together. It's a social gathering and also an opportunity for us to provide a market outlook and some educational training on relevant topics.

In the beginning, about a hundred people attended the event, but with each year it grew in popularity. People love the breakfast, the fellowship, the entertainment, and market outlook and look forward to coming each year.

The year 2019 will mark the twenty-second annual holiday event, an event where attendance has continued to dramatically tick higher and higher each year. Over the years, clients began to tell us that they enjoy meeting new people and seeing old friends, so we began scheduling other client events. It requires planning time and financial outlay, but we believe in investing in our clients' well-being and extending their social networks. It's just as important as talking to them about financial matters. These social gatherings especially serve the networking needs of our clients who are widows and widowers.

One exercise that can be helpful when you retire is to sit down and make a list of the people who are most important to you, particularly those you haven't seen in a while: family, old school friends, college buddies, maybe mentors from earlier in your life. Take stock of who you know and who's been important to you through the years.

Retirement is the perfect time to get back in touch with those you've lost contact with over time, so make a list and reach out. It feeds into your social network.

Another way to expand your network is through mentoring. I've seen many professionals retire from engineering firms here in Kansas City over the last few years who are keeping their minds sharp by mentoring young engineers. My son, who attends the University of Missouri Science and Technology, has been mentored by several experienced engineers who've helped him chart his career path.

In fact, once you're retired, you can spend even more time researching, reading, and studying the subjects that interest you. You're not done learning, growing, or contributing. The best can be yet to come.

My mother lost my stepfather almost nine years ago in 2010, and I watched her walk through a long, difficult healing process. I firmly believe that a key to her healing was staying engaged in her social networks. I've seen the same in the lives of many clients. If and when you deal with the loss of a spouse or partner during retirement, the best thing you can do for yourself is to stay involved. Work as a volunteer, give back to your community, do the things that feed your soul. If there's a cause that is close to your heart, contribute your time to it. If you have a faith community, plug in and stay connected. We believe in this so much that we have initiated a Valentine's Day luncheon designed specifically for widows and widowers.

In fact, even now, as you are planning and preparing for retirement, I encourage you to keep a journal. Along with the names of those people you want to reconnect with in retirement, start brainstorming about organizations, charities, faith communities, hobbies, or mentorship opportunities you can get involved with.

Do you want to run a marathon? Write it down. Have you always dreamed of seeing the pyramids in Egypt? Write it down. Jot down all of your ideas, so that when you retire, you will have no lack of ideas. Your calendar is going to open up, and opportunities are going to start coming your way.

IT'S YOUR TIME NOW

One nice thing about retirement is that you have more choice about who you spend time with. When you were working full-time, you had to interact with coworkers every day, whether you liked them or not. Now, your time is your own, and you don't have to feel guilty about it. In retirement you get to choose which social networks you want to be involved in. Feel free to disengage with places, people, and circumstances that don't suit you. This is your life to live.

LEARN TO SAY NO

The minute people hear you're retired, they're going to start asking you to do things. You might be invited to join multiple charity boards. You will be asked to babysit. You will be asked to do many things, and if you're not careful, other people's priorities will consume all of your time.

Learn the art of saying no to anything you don't want to be part of, especially if you are a people pleaser. It doesn't take much to get stretched too thin, and if that happens, it compromises the whole purpose of your retirement, which is to enjoy your life to the fullest. You may also be asked to lend money or support a family member or friend.

An easy way to guard against getting overcommitted is to never give an answer right away when you're asked to do something. Always buy time. "Let me sleep on it," you might say. This is important because some of the things you get invited to will be flattering. It's an honor when organizations want your time and commitment, but that doesn't mean you should do it.

When it comes to lending money or providing long-term financial support for a friend or child, consider using your financial advisor as the "bad guy." We play this role for clients who have a hard time saying no even when they may be compromising their own retirement security by loaning money or providing support. In any of these cases, carefully think about any request before giving an answer.

You don't want to go from the stress of working every day to the stress of being overcommitted in retirement. It happens more often than people realize. After the work you've done, the assets you've built up, and the discipline you've shown in practicing delayed gratification, you deserve to enjoy your retirement free of guilt.

Chapter Thirteen

TEND TO YOUR MARRIAGE

I've counseled and coached thousands of people into their retired life, and I've seen the things that have worked, and the things that haven't. One of the most common challenges—one that is often unexpected—is tending to marriage as a retired person.

You've never been retired before, so it's a new experience. Maybe you've been married for decades, but you've never been *married and retired*. Throughout your professional life, you've learned how to respond to job loss, market corrections, health problems, family troubles, and professional challenges, but when the full-time job ends and you find yourself spending all day, every day, with your spouse, it's a new experience.

You've spent years practicing discipline in order to prepare for retirement. It would be a shame to finally get there and then watch your relationship start to fail, but it happens. I've seen it far too many times. We call it *gray divorce*, and it's more common today than ever.

AVOIDING GRAY DIVORCE

These tensions typically start to appear in the six months leading up to retirement. Suddenly, each spouse starts expressing anxiety about what retired life will be like. Differing opinions on what that life should look like start to become obvious.

We always check in with people three to four months after retirement to make sure they are adjusting well. Often, we'll find that the spouse who worked full-time is having a bit of a problem. The other spouse might say, "Well, we're trying to get him or her to get out of the house and do some things, but they haven't gotten around to it yet."

The tension is usually palpable at this point, because both spouses are locked up in the house together. They might not be angry at each other, but they are struggling to deal with the constant close quarters. They're used to one or both of them going off to work every weekday. With the work routine gone, they're trying to figure out how to fill the time.

If left to fester, this situation can turn into resentment, so it's better to deal with it right away. A successful transition is always based on communication, so it's important for couples to talk about what they are retiring *to*, rather than merely discussing what they are retiring *from*.

These conversations can be energizing, because it gives spouses an opportunity to begin envisioning a happy future. Maybe they decide to join the local YMCA, or the community center, or a club. Maybe they decide simply to get outside and take regular walks. Working on being healthy together can be a powerful bonding experience, and it's something many married couples just don't have time to work on before retirement. By exercising together, you're firing off endorphins and sharing an experience that brings you closer together.

INDEPENDENCE AND MEETING IN THE MIDDLE

We've found that the healthiest retired couples spend a lot of time together, but also a little time apart on a regular basis. This allows each person to have their own interests. It's important to discuss how this dynamic will work best.

In most cases, we recommend that you spend three days a week going your separate ways during the day. Each spouse can pursue their individual interests on those days, whether it's a hobby, volunteer work, or sport. Make it a routine, so you can get into the rhythm of your new life.

A couple who recently retired had been clients of ours for years. The husband loved to play golf with his two sons, and he was looking forward to many rounds of golf during retirement. His wife, however, had a passion for travel, and she was looking forward to seeing a lot of interesting places in her retirement.

In discussing this with them, we came up with a great compromise. As part of their retirement plan, they joined a golf club and the wife took golfing lessons. The husband then agreed to travel with her all over the world, as long as they could play a little golf in some of the cool places they visited. As it turned out, this compromise proved to be a vital part of their retirement, and they are thriving.

Because they were willing to communicate and respect each other's interests, they were able to create a healthy dynamic that allowed both of them to pursue their passions.

My wife and I had a similar conversation. I'm a licensed pilot, and it's one of my true passions. We own a plane, and I love being able to fly it nationally to conduct business. It's a stress reliever, almost like a meditation. While it's not my wife's primary interest, she has met me halfway. She's taken a few flying lessons, and she's even landed the plane a few times with an instructor on board.

For my fiftieth birthday, her present to me was taking ten flying lessons so she can help when we go places together. She has met me in the middle, but I'm also meeting her in the middle. Unlike me, she's not interested in flying circles over Kansas City, taking a sky-high look at Arrowhead Stadium, then flying out over Lake of the Ozarks and back. She prefers visiting fun and interesting places, so when we fly, I ask her where she wants to go.

Every couple has to navigate these issues to some degree, but in retirement they become more pressing. It has been my privilege to see many couples successfully merge their interests and passions to create a new, healthy relationship dynamic in retirement.

GETTING YOUR FINANCES IN SYNC

Some couples don't realize how out of sync they are until they get into retirement. Suddenly, they find themselves struggling to agree on financial matters. Are we going to travel frequently or not? Are we going to stay here in the same city, or are we going to move closer to our children and grandchildren? It's amazing how many big issues like these aren't discussed until after retirement, when suddenly both spouses realize how off-base they are with each other.

Money creates more confusion, stress, and disagreement than just about anything else in a marriage, so we always recommend both spouses attend every meeting with their financial advisor. With both spouses present, we can see where each one is coming from, what their individual histories are, what drives and inspires them, and how they each see their lives going forward.

It's much better to get those out-of-sync expectations on the table when you're planning for retirement, so you can find your middle ground. I was meeting with a couple once when the husband mentioned that he wanted to do an around-the-world cruise. We priced it, and the cost came to about $105,000. When the wife heard that, she cringed. They could afford it, but since it wasn't her passion or interest, the cost seemed shockingly exorbitant to her. Learning this enabled us to discuss their options, so we could get them on the same page.

When we have these discussions with clients, we're also figuring out what they are going to live on each month, and where that money will come from. If we're managing their accounts, we will almost always withhold federal and state taxes for them and send money to their bank account on the day they've chosen to receive the funds each month. Of course, the spending plan we discussed earlier in the book comes into play at this point, because we want to make sure both spouses are on the same page in regard to their spending. When one spouse's spending is out of control, it becomes a huge source of conflict.

By having both spouses at the meeting with the financial advisor, they can both hear from the professional what needs to happen to make their financial plan work. We can work together to bring spending habits in line. That's much more effective than one spouse coming home and trying to explain it all to the other spouse.

These meetings are also a chance to make sure both spouses are on the same page with risk tolerance. One spouse might be fine investing in the stock market, creating a diversified portfolio of equities. They understand volatility, and they know that the markets will recover as long as they don't panic and sell at a bad time. However, the other spouse might know very little about investing in the stock market and might be uncomfortable with the idea. If we don't help them come to an agreement, it will create turmoil in the marriage.

Ideally, we want them both involved, we want both of them to understand the financial plan, and we want to find a middle ground that they are both comfortable with. This takes more than a single thirty-minute meeting and a pie chart. It requires rolling up the sleeves and having some in-depth conversations.

How important is this? In my experience, it can make or break a marriage.

The benefits go beyond marital bliss. At some point in the future, I know I will be sitting across the table from just one of the spouses. The other chair that used to be occupied at our meetings will be empty, but the work that both of them did together will ensure that the surviving spouse is taken care of. More than that, it will ensure that whichever spouse survives, they will know exactly where they stand because they were both involved in the process.

As a financial advisor, I've had the distinct privilege of

walking through life with so many wonderful people. I'm there through the good times, the bad times, and I've been there at the end of their lives. Being able to provide peace of mind for people throughout this trajectory has been a powerful experience for me, and I've endeavored to train my team to fully appreciate what they get to do. When you truly prepare for your retirement, it can become the most beautiful and moving phase of your life. It's worth all of the hard work.

CONCLUSION

If you listen to any of my *Keen On Retirement* podcasts, you will find that I routinely make the comparison between flight planning and retirement planning. In both instances, the stakes are high. It's fair to call them life-or-death endeavors.

If you've worked and saved a nest egg for forty years, you don't have forty more years to make it all back if you compromise your finances. In the same way, when you're up in the air and have a problem, you may have one shot to fix it. As a pilot, that's not something I take lightly. As a retiree, neither should you.

You might remember the tragic death of John F. Kennedy, Jr. Most people recall that he was flying his wife and her sister in his private plane at night to Martha's Vineyard, when they crashed into the ocean. Unless you have pilot training, however, you probably don't understand how it happened or why.

When you're flying on a clear-weather day, you can look outside and see the horizon, so you always know when your plane is level. However, when you fly into a cloud or on a dark night, suddenly your visibility is reduced to zero, and you can no longer depend on the horizon to orient your plane. In a car, there would be no way to safely navigate with zero visibility, but an airplane has instruments that help the pilot keep the plane right side up. One of the instruments is called the artificial horizon, and it's a lifesaver.

Flying with instruments requires a special instrument rating that is hard for pilots to get. Even after you earn it, you have to take ongoing training to maintain it and you have to stay current and proficient. Many private pilots are just flying for fun, so they never get the necessary training to earn their instrument rating.

When you're up in the air with zero visibility, your mind and body start to play tricks on you. It's a little like getting seasick on a boat. Suddenly, you can start to feel disoriented. The plane might be turning to the left, but the pilot feels like he's going to the right, so he turns farther to the left to correct his course. Suddenly, he's in a tight turn, and he's more disoriented than ever. This can happen in a matter of seconds, and if you don't have your instrument rating, you might not know it.

JFK Jr. didn't have an instrument rating, but in the United States, pilots are allowed to fly at night without an instrument rating as long as they can see by moonlight or lights on the ground. Ultimately, his crucial error was a decision he made to shave several minutes off his flight to Martha's Vineyard by cutting out across the ocean. If he had been flying up the coast, city lights below may have kept him oriented. Once he was out over the ocean, he found himself flying through a haze.

Suddenly, he lost visibility, so when the disorientation set in, he became confused. It is believed that it took less than a minute before he was so disoriented that he'd flipped the plane upside down without realizing it. When he pulled up to gain altitude, he inadvertently flew the plane into the ocean.

It might sound crazy if you've never flown a plane, but the disorientation that hits you when you have no visibility can be intense. You need to be able to read and fully trust your instruments under those conditions to survive.

DON'T FLY BLIND

I have obtained my instrument rating, and I would never

take off into clouds or haze if I didn't have the training, currency, and proficiency to rely on my instruments. I would never put myself, my passengers, or people on the ground at such risk—and it would be illegal.

In the same way, you should never fly blind in your financial life. When you do, you put yourself and your loved ones at risk. You have to understand what you're doing, so you can put a plan in place. It's your financial plan that becomes the artificial horizon in difficult times when you feel like you're flying blind. No matter what happens in the economy, in the political arena, in the markets, or with your health or the health of a loved one, your artificial horizon will keep you from making dangerous, knee-jerk decisions.

Having a solid fiduciary firm guiding you is like having Sully Sullenberger as your copilot, an expert who is trained to help you deal with even the most unexpected situations. It gives you someone you can trust on the journey, making it almost assured that you will arrive safely at your destination.

My goal with this book has been to create a practical manual of the things you should begin thinking about as you plan for retirement. There's simply no way to cover absolutely everything you need to know in one book, especially when each chapter could be a book unto itself. Rather than burying you in minutiae and details, I've chosen to provide you with a comprehensive view of the retirement horizon. If I have inspired you to begin thinking intentionally about these issues, then I've done my job.

MAP YOUR JOURNEY

As a follow-up exercise, I encourage you to get out a whiteboard and sit down with your spouse or partner, if you have one. Take a few hours to go through a blue-printing process, mapping out what you want your life to look like in three, five, ten, and twenty years. This is an exercise I always do with my wife. I write down what our ages will be at each of those time intervals, and what our children's ages will be, and we begin to think in specific terms about what life will look like. This is an exercise that takes time. You have to make it a priority and take time to do it right.

Use that whiteboard blueprint to clarify your vision for retirement. This is an opportunity your parents' and grandparents' generations didn't always get. Life expectancy was shorter, and there was very little planning. No one expected to live twenty or thirty years beyond retirement with decades of opportunity left for fulfillment.

Now, however, you can live your life to the fullest in

retirement—physically, mentally, spiritually, and financially—and "leave everything on the field." It's your life and your choice. Once you know how you want your life to be, you can reverse engineer a plan and financial engine to get there. Retirement should be a time of excitement and expectation about the next phase of your life.

LEARNING FROM MISTAKES

The fact that you're reading this book, that you've taken a real interest in getting ready for retirement, puts you ahead of the game. Most people approach retirement on autopilot, assuming everything will somehow magically fall into place. Worse yet, many try not to think about it.

They look up one day with retirement closing in and realize they don't have any money saved, and now their options are limited. If you've made some financial mistakes, it's nothing to feel guilty about. At least you're educating yourself and thinking about your future. Tough times are inevitable, but that's when character is built. As my pastor recently told me, "You can't have an inspirational testimony unless you've been tested in the hard times—no testimony without the test."

There's an exercise I like to do in seminars and small groups. I'll ask the group, "How do you learn?" One person might reply, "I learn visually." Another might say, "I learn through reading and study." Someone else might say, "I learn through experience." Those are all valid answers, but they're not the answer I'm looking for.

In a recent meeting, someone gave me the answer I'm always looking for: "I learn by making mistakes."

That's it. We learn by our mistakes.

I responded with a second question: "What kind of mistakes do we most learn from?" One person said, "The most painful." Another said, "The most expensive." I think those two answers hit the nail on the head. The most painful and expensive mistakes we make are the most impactful.

When I meet young people who are pouring their money into penny stocks or, worse yet, heading down to the casino here in Kansas City and trying to beat the house, I know the worst thing that could happen to them is that they win big. If they lose, they can learn and make smarter, more successful decisions in the future.

Having said that, let me add one caveat. If you're at the point of retirement and you've managed to save enough money, now is *not* the time to make an expensive mistake. Don't make an emotional decision. Don't trust your money to an inexperienced or unscrupulous advisor. Now is the time to make sure your money is invested intentionally and your retirement secure. You no longer have time to recover from an expensive mistake.

By staying engaged, learning, and taking advice from reputable financial advisors, you can get on track—and stay on track—for a happy, comfortable, and exciting retirement.

RETIREMENT RESOURCES

For more information on the topics covered in this book, check out our many free resources, including podcasts, articles, and tools, at KeenOnRetirement.com.

ACKNOWLEDGMENTS

I want to start by thanking my amazing wife, Carissa. Thank you, my love, for understanding how my brain works and for all of your patience over the last year and a half as this project came together. Your thoughts and opinions are always spot on and provide me with continual sanity checks. I could not have formulated this book without your love and support.

A special thanks goes to my children. Thanks to each of you for working hard and staking your claim and journey in life—and for allowing me to use our many stories about our lives in my blogs and podcasts. Your stories have been an inspiration for this book.

Thanks to Matt Wilson for coming my way seventeen years ago and for all of your hard work and determination in making Keen Wealth what it is today. Much of the journey related in this book included your meaningful contributions. I also thank you for your friendship and your willingness to always go the extra mile. The best is yet to come.

Thanks to Leslie Penka, our Chief Compliance Officer and VP of Operations at Keen Wealth Advisors. Thank you, Leslie, for joining our firm and keeping me on task and compliant in getting this project across the finish line.

Thanks to Tae Kim for having the faith to join the Keen Wealth team and for your work in editing the manuscript. Also, special thanks for using your professional photography skills to take the airborne pictures we used in the book. It's great to be working with you again.

Thanks to my entire team at Keen Wealth Advisors. You step up each and every day for our clients, and you gave me the faith to make this book happen. Thanks to all of you for looking high and low for my lost picture album from my time working in the World Trade Center. You are amazing team players, and I couldn't be prouder.

Thanks to Mark Wolf, who has mentored me with patience and love for nearly two decades. This would not have been possible without your faith in and commitment to me. You filled in the gaps and so much more.

Thanks to my flight instructors, Jim Rainen and Major Gen. Hank Canterbury. Thanks for letting me know when I need to be better—in some cases, not so gently—which I am immensely grateful for. Your instruction and care have made a meaningful impact on me as an aviator and in my thinking, both in life and as a financial advisor.

Thank you to Steve Sanduski, my good friend and podcast co-host. Your insight, expertise, sincerity, character, and friendship are priceless. Thank you for giving me the confidence to step up.

Thank you to Mark Moses for your friendship and guidance and for your focus and commitment on best practices in business and in life. You inspired me to make this happen.

Thank you to Jim Stowers III. First, for all of the amazing work you and your family have done and continue to do to make the world a better place, giving "Hope for Life." Second, thank you for taking the time to review my manuscript. Words cannot express how honored I am to have worked for you just out of college and to have now reconnected in this season of life.

Thank you, Joe Ratterman, for all of your flight mentoring and for taking the time to review my manuscript. I am very grateful for your friendship and guidance on all.

A special thanks to the late Mr. John Gioia, my economics teacher at Park Hill High School, who sincerely cared about training us on how to live in the world.

Thanks to Greg Nuzzo, who helped me open my first Schwab account when I was sixteen.

Thanks to Pastor Phillip O'Reilly for walking the walk and for your friendship and accountability.

To my mothers, Jean Curry and Irene Smith, my father, George William (Billy) Keen, and my stepfather, Tom Curry, Grandpa Cecil and Grandma Letha Keen, Grandpa Master Sergeant Pat and Grandma Mary Lowe, and my Great Aunt Nina K. Schantz. Each of you made a profound impact on me for which I am forever grateful.

Finally, a special thanks to my publishing team at Lioncrest for all of your professionalism and for keeping me on track throughout this process. This wouldn't have been possible without you.

ABOUT THE AUTHOR

BILL KEEN's interest in finances began at an early age when he was exposed to financial hardship. In his own words, "By age ten, I knew I would have to learn to understand saving and investing to be able to eventually assist my family." Even in high school, Bill was regularly on the pay phone between classes checking his stock positions. In 1985, while working as a health club attendant, he met a senior executive at a major airline who introduced him to the markets and helped him open his first investment account. Though young, he quickly realized that if he pursued that knowledge, he could impart this knowledge on others, especially those dealing with financial hardship like his own family.

As founder and CEO of Keen Wealth Advisors, Bill's desire was to build one of the country's most personal and trusted wealth and retirement advisory firms. He brings twenty-seven years of experience to the table.

He is regularly asked to share his thinking with national media outlets such as *U.S. News and World Report*, *Reuters*, *The Wall Street Journal*'s *Market Watch*, and *Yahoo! Finance*. He also co-hosts *Keen On Retirement*, a podcast designed to provide Keen Wealth Advisors' friends and clients with an additional tool to stay informed and educated on key issues related to retirement planning and investing.

Bill is a board member for Angel Flight Central, a volunteer non-profit organization with a mission of serving people in need by arranging charitable flights for healthcare or other humanitarian purposes. Since its founding in 1995, over four hundred volunteer pilots have donated their time and planes to fly over nine million miles to serve over twenty-six thousand passengers in need. Bill has also served on the board of the Children's Center for the Visually Impaired, a Kansas City-based organization that helps children with visual impairment reach their highest potential in a sighted world.

Bill's other philanthropic causes include the Boys and Girls Club of America, Camp Quality Kansas, Camp Quality Missouri, Exodus Cry, Kansas District Optimists, and the AOPA.

He is a supporter of the cycling community and the title sponsor for the Big D Cycling team, as well as a contributor to the Kansas Cycling Association. The Big D

Cycling team competes throughout the US and participates in bicycle rodeos to conduct helmet fittings and bicycle repair for children in the local community. In 2013, along with The Kansas Cycling Association (KCA), Bill announced "The Keen Wealth Cup," a traveling trophy that is awarded to the cycle team with the best overall record in the KCA Kansas Best All-Around Rider (KBAR) Series for a given year.

Bill and his wife, Carissa, reside in the Kansas City area where they enjoy the outdoors and the joys that come from having a blended family of five children. An avid aviator, Bill is an instrument-rated private pilot carrying high performance, high altitude, and complex endorsements. He is also a member of the Malibu/M-Class Owner and Pilots Association and regularly flies his Piper Meridian to various destinations around the country.

Bill greatly enjoys the personal aspect of Keen Wealth Advisors. He considers each client a friend.

He obtained a Bachelor of Science in Business Administration from the University of Central Missouri and has lectured on investing at the University of Missouri Bloch School of Business graduate program, as well as many major corporations in the Kansas City area. He also holds the Chartered Retirement Planning Counselor℠ designation.

Made in the USA
Lexington, KY
06 September 2019